Krautrock

Krautrock

Marshall Gu

BLOOMSBURY ACADEMIC
NEW YORK • LONDON • OXFORD • NEW DELHI • SYDNEY

BLOOMSBURY ACADEMIC
Bloomsbury Publishing Inc
1385 Broadway, New York, NY 10018, USA
50 Bedford Square, London, WC1B 3DP, UK
29 Earlsfort Terrace, Dublin 2, Ireland

BLOOMSBURY, BLOOMSBURY ACADEMIC and the Diana logo
are trademarks of Bloomsbury Publishing Plc

First published in the United States of America 2024
Reprinted 2024

Library of Congress Cataloging-in-Publication Data
Names: Gu, Marshall, author.
Title: Krautrock / Marshall Gu.
Description: [1st.] | New York : Bloomsbury Academic, 2023. | Series:
Genre: a 33 1/3 series | Includes bibliographical references and index. |
Summary: "Explores this far-reaching German-based genre beyond its
biggest names, emphasizing just how wide its breadth was leading
up to and during the 1970s"– Provided by publisher.
Identifiers: LCCN 2023009998 (print) | LCCN 2023009999 (ebook) |
ISBN 9798765103296 (paperback) | ISBN 9798765103302 (ebook) |
ISBN 9798765103319 (pdf) | ISBN 9798765103326 (ebook other)
Subjects: LCSH: Krautrock (Music)–History and criticism. |
Popular music–Germany–1971–1980–History and criticism.
Classification: LCC ML3534.6.G3 G85 2023 (print) | LCC ML3534.6.G3
(ebook) | DDC 781.660943/09047—dc23/eng/20230301
LC record available at https://lccn.loc.gov/2023009998
LC ebook record available at https://lccn.loc.gov/2023009999

ISBN: PB: 9798765103296
       ePDF: 9798765103319
       eBook: 9798765103302

Series: Genre: A 33 1/3 Series

Typeset by RefineCatch Limited, Bungay, Suffolk
Printed and bound in the United States of America

To find out more about our authors and books visit www.bloomsbury.com
and sign up for our newsletters.

Contents

Acknowledgements

Thank you to my family Yin Tan, Jessica Gu, and Hans Kleiner, for your support. Thank you to all my friends for your encouragement. Thank you to my partner Kristina Seefeldt, and our puppy Pepper, for all your love.

Thank you to everyone at Bloomsbury for helping make this dream a reality. Thank you Leah Babb-Rosenfield, Goretti Crowley, and Merv Honeywood. Thank you Ryan Pinkard for your patience and helping me edit this book.

Thank you to the music writers and journalists who wrote tirelessly about krautrock. Thank you Ulrich Adelt, Julian Cope, Jan Reetze, and David Stubbs, for writing informative books about the genre.

Thank you to the Tone Glow family who helped shape me into a better writer. Thank you Joshua Minsoo Kim for responding to a DM all those years ago.

And of course, thank you to these musicians in the first place for making all this wonderful music. Thank you Lutz Graf-Ulbrich, Marja Burchard, and Ax Genrich for speaking with me.

Introduction

Krautrock Is Not a Music Genre: Krautrock Is a Way of Life

That is the conclusion that I've come to while writing this book about its most famous bands. Music genres have defining characteristics, and we as listeners group artists and their outputs into different genres based on those features. The many musicians that made music that would be called krautrock come from the same place (Germany) and time (between the late '60s and late '70s), but time and place do not describe what krautrock sounds like.

What does krautrock actually sound like? It can sound like the most unrelenting psychedelia you've ever heard. It can sound like the most hypnotic grooves found in rock music. It can sound like jazz, like junk, like pure noise, or like peaceful ambient music. It can sound like nothing you've ever heard before, which was certainly the original mission statement of many of its practitioners—to reject the sound of the American and British bands that came before them.

Some music journalists, scholars, and writers have pointed out loose threads connecting some krautrock bands, such as the motorik beat, the psychedelic atmosphere, the embrace of electronic instruments and other new technologies. But compare any two major krautrock bands, and you will see how these are not shared traits. Neu! had a motorik beat, but Faust did not. Amon Düül II were heavily psychedelic, but Cluster were not. Kraftwerk made heavy use of synthesizers, but Can did not. Can made use of the studio as an instrument to edit songs, but Embryo did not. The list goes on. Ultimately, krautrock's sonic diversity means that people interested in the genre cannot so easily queue up a playlist without expecting stylistic twists and turns. It is a genre that works best on a band-by-band basis, which is how this book is structured.

All this is to say, krautrock bands do not share common characteristics, but instead share in the common culture of postwar Germany. Most of krautrock's musicians were born in Germany right after the Second World War. Because of Hitler's policies around music and the Allied occupation of Germany immediately after the war, there was a distinct lack of German musical culture, especially when compared to countries such as the United States or United Kingdom. And so these musicians made their own from scratch.

Where does the term "krautrock" come from? According to Faust's Jean-Hervé Péron, the word was created by the label Virgin Records, which was on the lookout for a new sound from Germany. According to others, it was the British music press who coined the term—it has been attributed to the famous British disc jockey John Peel and to the music magazine *Melody Maker*. But no matter the story of origin, it wasn't a German who came up with the term. Given that the word "Kraut" is a derogatory slur—derived from sauerkraut—made up by the Allies against the Germans, this is not surprising.

If you were to ask some of these bands what they think about being called krautrock, they would likely scoff at the term. In an interview with Steve Hanson, Can singer Damo Suzuki claimed to never have made krautrock.[1] Amon Düül II guitarist John Weinzierl stated clearly that the band was not a krautrock band.[2] Guru Guru drummer Mani Neumeier never liked the word, saying, "It was a label put upon us by others like 'Oh, now the Krauts even want to make rock music.'"[3] With such a stupid genre name, who could blame these artists for distancing themselves from it?

When I spoke to Lutz Graf-Ulbrich, guitarist of the band Agitation Free, and Marja Burchard, now-leader of the band Embryo, both shared similar views, which is that the origin of the term was originally conceived to put down Germans. But overtime, what began as an insult to German music would eventually morph into what is today regarded as a stamp of authenticity, thanks in part to musicians such as David Bowie and Brian Eno, who helped popularize it outside of Germany.

Strangely enough, not all krautrock rocks very much if at all: the name is a misnomer in that regard. And when it does, it is certainly not with the same rhythmic backbone that makes up so much American and British rock. Some may argue that a defining feature of krautrock is what would be known as the "motorik beat." *Motorik* is the German word for "motor skill," and the motorik beat refers to a tightly regimented 4/4 cadence that was used by bands such as Neu!, and Can sounds very much like a locomotive on the move. The thing is, only a handful of krautrock bands really used the motorik beat—most didn't.

On a superficial level, krautrock has a cerebral aspect in the way it mixes world music, avant-garde classical, and free jazz elements into a rock format, a point that was capitalized on when trying to market some of these bands. The record label that was responsible for releasing many of krautrock's most important bands was called Brain, founded by Bruno Wendel and Günter Körber, who left Rolf-Ulrich Kaiser's Ohr label just before it folded. The cover of Can's *Tago Mago*, one of krautrock's most enduring albums, depicts an orange silhouette that is a cross between a mushroom (referencing the drug, the bomb, and one of the songs therein) and a person's head with a very large brain. In the 2000s, Target Music released a series of krautrock compilations subtitled *Music for Your Brain*. However, once again, not all krautrock is cerebral. Most of it is, in fact, the opposite: anti-cerebral, primal.

By the late '70s, most of the original and more daring krautrock groups had called it a day, while the ones that remained spun their wheels to a thinning audience. But krautrock maintains its relevance decades later: reissues and unearthed live performances are still being released to enthusiastic new audiences, while the genre has had long-lasting influence on countless other genres, including punk, indie rock, electronic, and ambient. Albums by Can, Faust, and Neu! are consistently placed on lists of the best albums of the 1970s, where these strange, avant-garde, and foreign records find themselves ranked next to far more popular American and British albums from artists such as Fleetwood Mac, Pink Floyd, and Stevie Wonder.

Despite the name, its anti-Anglo-American philosophy, and its penchant for long, thoroughly uncommercial songs, krautrock managed the impossible: it broke out of Germany. First, some bands found unlikely success in the UK, more success than they found at home in many cases. And then slowly, krautrock crossed the Atlantic and found an audience in North America, before eventually reaching listeners as far away as Japan and Australia. For myself, a Chinese Canadian who discovered Can as a young adult, krautrock was the coolest thing I'd ever heard—and it still is.

Ultimately, krautrock is a gateway, not just into these electrifying new sounds that were not being made in other countries, but into German culture. Because one key to understanding krautrock is the political context that created it in the first place.

Degenerate Music

While the first krautrock bands formed in the late 1960s, krautrock's story begins far earlier: with the Third Reich. For a country's dictator, Adolf Hitler was deeply invested in the arts, or at least, a version of it that fit his specific ideals. Everything else was labeled *entartet* ("degenerate"). *Entartete kunst* ("degenerate art") and *entartete musik* ("degenerate music") was not limited to the creations of Jewish artists as often thought. Hitler also loathed modernity and the avant-garde, considering them dangerous and un-German. The Nazis suppressed such expressions by imposing sanctions on German artists, confiscating works, and going so far as to host the notorious Entartete Kunst exhibitions that denounced them by way of displaying them in shame.

In a 1934 speech, Hitler specifically called out the Futurists and Dadaists as "spoilers of art," and so one can only imagine the fright he would have had if he had heard krautrock.[4] Bands like Can, Embryo, and Faust all used Dadaist mantras in their lyrics or images. Notably, Dada was an art movement that arose in direct reaction to the horrors of the First World War, such that there was no wonder why krautrock bands reacting to the Second World War would find inspiration in it. Meanwhile, bands like Kraftwerk and the practitioners of the closely related Berlin School were Futurist in their embrace of the machine. This was especially the case with Kraftwerk, whose special interests in speed and modernity aligned with that of Futurism's founder Filippo Tommaso Emilio Marinetti. And if not Dadaist or Futurist, most of the bands discussed in this book are avant-garde with no interest in the traditional aesthetics of the previous century that Hitler cherished.

Furthermore, krautrock bands did not have any consideration for keeping their music "pure." Whereas Nazi authorities thought of jazz music as one of the most degenerate types of music, musicians in the bands Can, Embryo, Guru Guru, and even Kraftwerk all had jazz backgrounds.[5] In fact, Embryo are essentially a jazz fusion band that traveled across the world, collaborating with other musicians from other countries and incorporating the sounds from those cultures into their own version of krautrock; they were the antithesis of White, nationalist rock music, having largely abandoned rock music altogether early on. Similarly, Can incorporated music like funk, jazz, reggae, and disco into a sound that was also informed by the German avant-garde composer Karlheinz Stockhausen. Moreover, two of Can's lead singers were musicians of color. A decade ahead of the "world music" market that was popularized by artists such as Talking Heads, Paul Simon, and Peter Gabriel, krautrock bands such as these were absorbing global music styles for their own, unique vision.

Meanwhile, a band like Neu!, which had neither jazz nor world influences, made a political statement their own way. As the drummer of Neu!, Klaus Dinger invented the motorik beat (that he called the Apache beat), which took on its own life and its own meaning, symbolizing a way for Germany to move forward, out of the musical void created by Hitler. Whether these bands made these anti-Nazi decisions consciously is ultimately irrelevant: simply by being anti-conservative and anti-xenophobic, their music was inherently anti-Nazi.

After the War

Shortly after Adolf Hitler's suicide, the Nazis officially surrendered to the Allies, marking the end of World War II in Europe on midnight May 8, 1945. But the first years after the war were devastatingly harsh for the German people, who lacked basic infrastructure due to Allied bombings. English writer and explorer Douglas Botting stated in his book, *In the Ruins of the Reich*, that "Not one of the country's great cities had escaped the destruction brought about by the air-bombing and the land-fighting."[6] Over twenty million Germans were rendered homeless. Many of the men that would have been tasked to help rebuild the country were crippled or killed during the war, while others were displaced or held abroad as prisoners of war.[7]

There was also a food shortage as a result of the war. Food rationing, already in place by Hitler for the war effort, was further restricted.[8] The food ration card promised a maximum of 1,550 calories per person, not that it mattered since there was no food available to begin with, as food production had dropped by 50 percent.[9] There were times after the war when only 800 calories were doled out, and so people resorted to stealing or prostitution to survive.[10] The winter between 1946 and 1947 would turn out to be one of the coldest of the century, nicknamed the "Hungerwinter." With no fuel to heat homes, 352 people died from hypothermia in Berlin alone, and another 55,000 had to be treated for frostbite. Malnourished and living in impoverished conditions, others succumbed to diseases like tuberculosis and typhoid, which sharply rose among Germany's population.

Beyond physical needs, there was also the mental component. This great nation was now divided into four zones, each occupied by a different foreign power, and left to the mercy of its conquerors: Russia claimed East Germany; America occupied the south; Britain occupied the northwest; and France occupied the southwest. Berlin was similarly divided into four corresponding zones.

The reichsmark, the German currency from 1924 to 1948, had become worthless thanks to over-circulation, and so people resorted to bartering instead.[11] In particular, using cigarettes had notable practical qualities for trade including being small, transportable, and countable, with the added benefit of being an appetite suppressant.[12] Black markets also developed, where townsfolk could trade in their valuables for luxury items, like coffee and white bread, brought in from the Occupation armies.

On September 28, 1944, US President Dwight D. Eisenhower proclaimed, "In the area of Germany occupied by the forces under my command we shall obliterate Nazism and German militarism. We shall overthrow the Nazi rule, dissolve the Nazi party and abolish the cruel, oppressive and discriminatory laws and institutions which the party has created."[13] They would soon learn that denazification was easier said than done: the Nazi Party totaled twelve million members, and ex-Nazis had moved from positions of power within the Schutzstaffel (the SS) to other positions of power, from the police force and the Bundesnachrichtendienst (the BND, the West German secret service), to other civil services and beyond. Attempts to root out Nazis failed when it was clear that many had experience and expertise that could not be easily replaced. To add to this, the majority of the German population were unaware or unconvinced of the wrongdoings of Nazis.

In 1948, US Secretary of State George C. Marshall advocated to restore the economies of the European countries after the war. Under the European Recovery Program, better known as the Marshall Plan, the United States provided monetary aid to Europe in an effort to slow the spread of communism. Of the $13.9 billion (approximately $170 billion when adjusted to inflation) that the United States sent to Europe, $1.4 billion, or 10 percent, was given specifically to West Germany.[14]

At the same time, Ludwig Erhard, recently nominated to the Director of Economics at the Bizonal Economic Council and later, briefly, Chancellor of West Germany, began a multipronged approach to rebooting Germany's economy. First, there was the currency reform of 1948, where he was instrumental in replacing the worthless reichsmark with the deutsche mark. Erhard also lowered taxes from the Nazis' original 85 percent tax rate to 18 percent, in an effort to promote spending. The results of the Marshall Plan and Erhard's policies were referred to as *die Wirtschaftswunder*, or "the economic miracle," which swiftly increased Germany's production levels while putting an end to the bartering and black-market systems.

Over the next decade, despite the major economic upswing, the shadow of the war and Nazi Germany lingered. The new generation—including the ones that would grow up and form krautrock bands—understood that something terrible had happened, but they had no clear way of knowing exactly what. There were no archives, and the older generation kept quiet when asked about what they had seen or done. Agitation Free's Lutz Graf-Ulbrich, who grew up in Berlin in the 1950s, recalls that in school, history classes only went up to the 1920s. Similarly, in an interview with *Perfect Sound Forever*, Amon Düül II guitarist John Weinzierl recalled that,

> In the sixties in Germany, we had a very special generation conflict. The generation before us experienced the Nazis and

war times. After the war, there was a completely different political climate, but in many institutions, the old smell was still present. Children asked their parents about the big war and their role in it, students asked their teachers, and it was hard to get proper answers.[15]

This led to a heavily politicized new generation. By the late 1960s, the counterculture movement in Germany paralleled what was happening across the ocean in America. Many student protests took place to reject current affairs, including nuclear arms and the Vietnam War, but in Germany, the scope expanded to include the silence, traditionalism, and remaining Nazism in the country.

It didn't help that schlager—the popular music of the day in Germany—translating to "Hits")—was fiercely apolitical. Instead, its lyrics were romantic and sentimental, if not saccharine, which brought the ire of many critics and the new generation of listeners, even though schlager remains popular to this day. Other European countries have their own versions of schlager, and indeed, some of the most famous schlager singers were decidedly not German (for example, a pre-ABBA Agnetha Fältskog). In those countries, pop songs such as these would have been regarded as harmless, but in the context of postwar Germany, some critics felt schlager was the opposite: a willful and, indeed, harmful forgetting of what the country had just gone through. It was condemned as *volksverdummerung*, or "brainwashing."

When krautrock bands talk about the "cultural void" that they came from, this is what they mean. Yes, there was different music abroad. There was jazz and schlager and rock and roll on the radio. But there wasn't a culture that was distinctly German. A lot of popular schlager was covers of British and American songs, while on the rock front, the Rattles—one of Germany's most successful rock groups—started the same way, covering music that wasn't German and singing the words in English, even if they had no idea what they meant. Kraftwerk member Ralf Hütter once said, "We woke up in the late '60s and realised that Germany had become an American colony … There was no German culture, no German music, nothing. It was like living in a vacuum. The young people were into the American way of living; cars, hamburgers and rock n' roll. Germany had lost its identity. We all felt very lost."[16]

One of the earliest krautrock bands, Xhol Caravan, embodies this quest to forge a unique identity and reject the American values that were thrust upon Germany. Before they were Xhol Caravan, they were a half-German, half-American Motown band formed in Wiesbaden called Soul Caravan, created to entertain the American soldiers stationed there by playing the music that the GIs wanted to hear. While its co-founders were both German, its front men were both American, as was their drummer. After releasing one generic R&B album in 1967—*Get in High*—they ditched the Motown sound, along with their American singers, and embraced free improvisation, joining the changing of the guard and becoming Xhol Caravan: a German band, playing German music.

Around the same time that these German bands were forming and recording their debut albums, British rock bands were on their own mission to have their art be taken as seriously as classical and jazz music, bridging the divide from what was perceived as "low art" (rock music) to "high art" (classical and jazz). In 1967, the Beatles and the Who both released concept albums, where individual songs are linked thematically or conceptually, and the albums were meant to be played as one single unit rather than a collection of disparate works. Soon, progressive rock further expanded what rock could be by incorporating complex time signatures, more common in classical music, as well as jazz's tricky improvisations. Where early rock music was criticized for its simplicity, progressive rock sought to abandon the three-chord approach. While this worked in the short-term—progressive rock became very popular in the early 1970s, exemplified by Pink Floyd's *The Dark Side of the Moon* being among the best-selling albums of all-time—it backfired in the long-run when audiences and critics began regarding the genre's ambitions as pretentious and overwrought.

Certainly, the krautrock bands felt that way. In contrast to what the prog rock bands were doing, krautrock bands did the exact opposite: they burrowed harder into rock's three-chord setup, with some bands such as Can repeating those chords for as long as their recording equipment would allow. By pushing rock's core elements to their absolute limit, many of these bands reached something avant-garde. The reasoning from these bands was different. Whereas progressive rock was an attempt to make rock music sound like "high art," krautrock bands internally reasoned that "high art" and "low art" were, in fact, one and the same. Whereas prog rock's lyrics became fanciful, poetic, and conceptual, krautrock did not care for lyricism at all, often resorting to Dadaist mantras or not deploying vocals at all. Whereas prog rock enjoyed technical precision of its instrumentalists, certain krautrock bands held the view that you did not need to know how to play your instrument well to play well. Whereas prog rock strove for perfection, krautrock knew there was no such thing. Perhaps the best illustration of krautrock's distaste of prog rock is when Xhol Caravan changed their name to simply "Xhol," partly to avoid any confusion with the British prog band Caravan.

Interestingly, very few krautrock bands emphasized either the melody or the rhythm. By contrast, the focal point of popular rock bands from the United States or Britain was the melody, supplied by the vocalist or the lead instrument. Meanwhile, the rhythm section of these bands only existed to serve the central melody. Even Neu!, influential because of their drum beat, was the result of balancing tension between its two members, one playing melody and the other playing rhythm; increase the mix of one or the other, and the band's hypnotic balance would be lost.

Jaki Liebezeit, the seemingly multiarmed drummer of the band Can, was expertly nimble on the kit, but in the actual music itself, his beats were no more important to the band's sound than Michael Karoli's guitar, or Damo Suzuki's voice, or Holger Czukay's bass. Thus, the rock beat, the guitar riff, the vocals, and the bass groove were treated as equal in krautrock, opting instead to have listeners focus on the interplay between the instruments. Krautrock, then, represents a mirror of what happened in German politics: after the fall of the Third Reich came democracy. In many krautrock bands, no one musician was more important than another.

Part of emphasizing texture and de-emphasizing text came out of necessity as krautrock did not have access to conventionally great singers. Can vocalist Damo Suzuki rarely communicated range or power, two metrics commonly used in describing great vocalists. In fact, you would often have to strain to make out the words at all. Likewise, Klaus Dinger who took up singing on the third Neu! record, only sounded good in the context of the proto-punk music that meshed with his coarse vocals. He was liberating, specifically *because* he was untrained. A noteworthy anecdote is when Can first looked to replace original vocalist Malcolm Mooney, they tested out American vocalist Lee Gates. While Gates was a technically better singer than Mooney, he possessed none of the same qualities that worked well in the confines of the band. It was a paradox: to be a great singer in krautrock, you had to not be a great singer.

This concept extended beyond just vocals. Notably, Amon Düül and Kluster—earlier incarnations of the bands Amon Düül II and Cluster—revolved around this notion that anyone could play music. To watch Amon Düül perform was to watch a group of mostly amateur musicians, some of whom had never been musically trained because Amon Düül was initially a commune, and everyone was encouraged to participate. Meanwhile, Kluster founder Conrad Schnitzler was a student of German artist Joseph Beuys, who proposed that "everybody is an artist," but Schnitzler honed in on that concept and applied it to music: "anybody can be a musician," his bandmate Moebius recalled in an interview with *Red Bull Academy*.[17] As another example, Tangerine Dream's Peter Baumann has said he considers himself a poor keyboard player.[18] You see similar sentiments across krautrock, which was part of the point: the freedom to play however you wanted allowed these musicians to create new sounds, informed by feeling and uninhibited by perceptions of right and wrong.

At the same time, unlike the hypermasculine hard rock that became increasingly popular as the '70s progressed, krautrock felt distinctly unmasculine by comparison. For one thing, there was less of a hierarchical structure in krautrock bands. Notably, there was rarely a front man or a lead vocalist, nor any great emphasis on sex appeal. In an extreme example, Xhol Caravan had neither a vocalist nor a guitarist. Krautrock bands instead emphasized interplay and texture over a flashy solo, and some bands even embraced the ambient and quiet to the point that the music can be considered feminine to a degree, a point made by David Stubbs in *Future Days: Krautrock and the Building of Modern Germany*. (Alas, with some rare exceptions such as Amon Düül II's Renate Knaup, most krautrock practitioners were men.) A seemingly throwaway lyric from a Can song comes to mind. On "Bring Me Coffee or Tea," as singer Damo Suzuki searches across the English lexicon for simple rhymes, he lands on one that emphasizes the genre's femininity: "Bring me coffee or tea / Call me Penelope." To these bands, concepts such as nationality and masculinity seemed beneath them. Krautrock, then, was the anti-prog, the anti-nationalist, the anti-masculine, the anti-perfect music of underground Germany.

Krautrock Begins

Genres do not have set start and end dates. Typically speaking, by the time it is given a name, its seeds have already been planted. There is no agreed-upon date when krautrock started, but 1968 was a formative year thanks to the International Essen Song Days, a major festival held in Essen, West Germany. The festival not only featured international artists instrumental in inspiring krautrock's sound, including Frank Zappa, but also newly formed West German groups, including Amon Düül I, Tangerine Dream, and Guru Guru. The event was organized by music journalist Rolf-Ulrich Kaiser, who would go on to be the founder of several record labels specializing in krautrock such as Ohr, Pilz, and Cosmic Couriers, which would release the records of Tangerine Dream, Klaus Schulze, Popol Vuh, and Ash Ra Tempel. Meanwhile, at the Essen festival, music producer and publisher Peter Meisel signed a handful of artists that played there.

Using 1968 as the demarcation point has another benefit, as many of the most important albums that would influence krautrock came out the year before, including the debut albums of Pink Floyd and the Velvet Underground, as well as the Beatles' *Sgt. Pepper's Lonely Hearts Club Band* and *Magic Mystery Tour*, giving these records time to proliferate across borders and spark these German bands' imaginations. While, broadly speaking, many krautrock bands rejected overt American and British rock influences, many of them were still curious about the countercultural sounds from those countries. With the exception of *The Velvet Underground & Nico*, these records are considered classic psychedelic rock albums, and that druggy, hazy psychedelia unquestionably informed the records of Amon Düül I/II, early Embryo, and Guru Guru.

Holger Czukay—Can's bassist, engineer, editor, and mixer—had no interest in rock music until he heard the Beatles' "I Am the Walrus," while Tangerine Dream's name came from a misheard lyric in "Lucy in the Sky with Diamonds." In their days as the noise terrorist group Kluster, Cluster's Hans-Joachim Roedelius and Dieter Moebius claimed to have been listening to Jimi Hendrix and the Velvet Underground as they tried, in their own untrained way, to recreate the sounds they heard. The Velvet Underground would have a profound influence on Can, who, early on, imitated their minimalist-inspired noise, while the cover of Faust's second album, *So Far*, is modeled after the Velvet Underground's second album, *White Light/ White Heat*.

The Essen Song Days took place in the last week of September 1968. Just one year later, the debut albums of Can, Embryo, Amon Düül I, and Amon Düül II arrived. In their wake, many more bands began to sprout up, seemingly overnight, with an electrifying new sound. These bands were not limited to any one region or single major city in Germany. The spread of krautrock across Germany had practical explanations, as the country had no cultural capital after the war, given that Berlin was in the middle of the Soviet Zone even before the Wall was erected. Jan Reetze notes that other major German cities could not have emerged as a cultural hub in Berlin's place because Germany was divided into four zones, "American, British, French and Soviet occupied zones, and of course, every zone wanted to have its own center."[19] So instead of being isolated to one cultural capital, krautrock emerged simultaneously across the nation.

The contents of this book devote each chapter to a single krautrock band, arranged in such a way that we take a road trip across Germany. We start in the western city of Cologne to visit Can, and then drive north to Wümme for Faust. From there, we head northeast to Berlin to discover Cluster, Tangerine Dream, Ash Ra Tempel, and Agitation Free. Then we head southwest, first to the city of Heidelberg to catch Guru Guru, and then Munich to listen to Amon Düül II, Embryo, and Popol Vuh. Finally, our trip ends at Düsseldorf to experience Neu! and Kraftwerk.

This book is in no way a comprehensive guide on every krautrock band, but rather a select handful of bands that best represent the genre's rejection of traditionalism, Nazism, and the encroaching Americanism in their own unique ways. Much like how krautrock was a mostly underground phenomenon, writing on the subject has been similarly niche and, up until recently, the krautrock library is scant, despite its proponents agreeing on its broad influence beyond borders and time.

My intent with this book is to help make this alien concept of a foreign rock music more approachable to outsiders. Because we should be listening to krautrock. We'd be better for it: it would change our conceptions of what rock music can be. It would open our ears to a sound that could not have been made in America or Britain, and help us understand a culture that may not be our own.

1 Future Days: CAN

Origins

Unlike many of the musicians discussed in this book that were born after World War II, almost all of the founding members of the band Can were born before the war began. Born in 1937, keyboard player Irmin Schmidt has early recollections of the horrors of the war, including hiding in cellars during the Allied bombings. And so, if Can's music is chaotic, swarming, and strange, for Schmidt, it was because the war was not a distant memory.

Originally born in Berlin, Schmidt moved west to study music, where he made great strides in becoming a respected classical composer, conductor, and pianist, including receiving tutelage from German avant-garde composer Karlheinz Stockhausen who was teaching at the Rheinische Musikschule in Cologne.

In 1966, Schmidt took a trip to New York City to compete in the Dimitri Mitropoulos Conducting Competition. I do not think it is an overestimation to say that had Schmidt flown anywhere else, Can's music would be drastically different. In fact, there may never have been a Can at all. While in New York, he immersed himself in the extremely new modern classical movement that was starting there called "minimalism," which he eventually brought back to Germany—this movement would be one of the founding pillars of Can's music.

Minimalism is exactly what the title suggests, a stripping away and endless repetition in search of something deeply profound. To the uninitiated, minimalism might even sound silly at first, and that's certainly what Schmidt thought when he met Terry Riley, soon to be one of minimalism's most well-known composers (even referenced in the song title of the Who's "Baba O'Riley"). As Schmidt tells it,

> In 1966 I came to New York for the first time. I was sent by my professors for a conducting contest. But right at the start, I met Terry Riley. He had this strange little grotto in the Bowery. We sat there night after night, and he made me play "de dah de dah de dah de"... me on the piano and him on the sax. At first I thought this was totally stupid. The result was that I was thrown out of the contest, because I missed certain rehearsals. I met Steve Reich, and he was also doing the "de dah de dah de"... but he was different, he had just finished a tape-loop piece. I was fascinated.[1]

While in New York, Schmidt also absorbed funk via Sly & the Family Stone and James Brown, as well as the Velvet Underground, a band that merged minimalism with rock music and produced with this new, weird low art–high art hybrid. He would bring these sounds with him back to Germany when he co-founded Can.

If Can's music is hard to place, it is because of the eclectic influences that led to its creation. With its propulsive rhythm, it does not sound like the minimalism of Terry Riley or Steve Reich. Nor does it sound like the Velvet Underground. And while much of their music is groovy, it definitely does not sound like funk. Instead, Can's music is a synthesis of different traditions, merging the avant-garde with the mainstream, classical with popular music, funk with rock, the techniques of Karlheinz Stockhausen with that of American composers, to produce something that sounds like no one else. Even decades later, after other musicians including Portishead and Radiohead mined Can's music for inspiration, Can still sounds unique and singular.

The fact that the band comes from different walks of life added to their uniqueness. Like Schmidt, bassist Holger Czukay was also a student of Stockhausen. Czukay brought his pupil Michael Karoli with him into the band to be the guitarist, the youngest member of Can's founders and also the only one born after the war. Meanwhile, drummer Jaki Liebezeit had worked in free jazz groups before signing on to play in Can, and was deeply fascinated by the rhythmic patterns from the other corners of the world. To solidify the worldly fusion, original lead vocalist Malcolm Mooney was an African American sculptor who had moved to Germany, and he was eventually replaced by Japanese traveler Damo Suzuki during the band's most famous iteration.

Even in the post-Suzuki years, when they sounded completely different from their earlier incarnations, they brought in Ghanaian percussionist Rebop Kwaku Baah and Jamaican bassist Rosko Gee, both of whom had played in English prog rock group Traffic. This incorporation of different nationalities and styles—notably funk and jazz, and later reggae and disco—was particularly important because this was a group of mostly German youth that was rejecting Nazi ideals by merging Black music forms with the German high art techniques of Stockhausen. One can only imagine the disgust with which the Nazis would have regarded this artistic hybrid, without even mentioning the fact that Can had non-White members singing in the frontlines.

Through Can, these musicians were reclaiming a history that was eradicated by the Nazis. For example, Liebezeit's father was a primary school teacher who died during the war under mysterious circumstances, with Liebezeit recalling, "He also made music—keyboards and violin. But they told me that they forbade him to make music. After that, he disappeared. Probably played some jazz-like music, or dance music. He didn't play the right music, anyway. A lot of music was forbidden at the time."[2] Meanwhile, Holger Czukay, originally born in the Free City of Danzig, now known as the city of Gdańsk in northern Poland, was originally born under the Dutch name "Schüring" but his father changed the family name as a means of evading the Nazis. It was not until 1968, and the formation of Can, that he changed his name back to Czukay.[3]

While Can's songs all sound like the natural product of a band working in sync and recorded in a single take, there is actually subtle tape manipulation happening on their records. In that regard, Holger Czukay's ability to chop up and splice together different takes while still sounding like a single organism was as vital to the band's sound as his bass playing, if not more so, especially since they only had access to primitive multitrack overdub technology. In Alan Warner's 33 1/3 book on *Tago Mago*, he likens their studio music to movies: "it produces the myth of being a seamless flow of 'real time,' but this is the illusion of continuity. It is not a record of 'real time' sounds at all but is built up and constructed out of smaller sections of different performances."[4]

If Czukay's ability to edit and overdub tapes was Can's secret weapon, the band's not-so-secret weapon was their drummer, Jaki Liebezeit. Liebezeit's drumming is metronomic yet tricky, subtle yet propulsive. There are times when it is so fast, yet technically precise, that you would believe he's a machine. Except Liebezeit also has a deeply empathetic sense of what the song and his bandmates required, something that a robot cannot replicate. It's no surprise that Liebezeit held a deep love for jazz legend Art Blakey, who shared many similar qualities and loved to champion the other musicians that he worked with and mentored. Liebezeit was also deeply curious about music from other countries, which started after he was introduced to Indian music in 1961, leading to his studies of the rhythms in African, Turkish, and Iranian music.[5]

Before he played jazz, Liebezeit was already familiar with rock music by playing the then-popular "beat music" for the entertainment of American soldiers stationed in Kassel. As a jazz player later on, Liebezeit had once played with Chet Baker, and then in free jazz outfits, which he eventually grew disillusioned with.[6] "When Can started I was finished with free jazz. I was not satisfied, they were not satisfied with me. In free jazz there was no future, everything was destroyed. Repetition was not allowed, but for me, repetition was one of the basic elements in music," he said.[7] Can's music—informed by the repetitive nature of the American minimalists—gave Liebezeit an opportunity to truly be free.

Early Years

Can recorded songs for their first album, intended to be called *Prepared to Meet Thy Pnoom*, but when they could not get a record company to bite, they continued to write new material. Eventually titled *Monster Movie*, their 1969 debut album would end up being the only studio album with Malcolm Mooney on vocals the entire way through until their brief reunion in the late '80s. The cover depicts a faceless Galactus, a cosmic giant from the Marvel Comics who has to consume planets to sustain himself, which Rob Young and Irmin Schmidt liken to

Can's assimilation with all different varieties of music in their book, *All Gates Open: The Story of Can*.[8]

The music of *Monster Movie* is appropriately large, lumbering, and ominous. "Yoo Doo Right" is a twenty-minute behemoth that is clearly in the model of the Velvet Underground's "Sister Ray," in that both songs run for absurd amounts of time, and gives the impression that Can would have kept going if only a single vinyl side could contain more music. All four songs on *Monster Movie* are heavy psychedelic rock, emphasized by Mooney's unhinged vocals as he sings puzzling lyrics of a father who "hasn't been born yet" and a woman who "smoked a haiku cigarette." Meanwhile, before he joined Can, Michael Karoli was only an acoustic guitar player, and so he leans hard into electric guitar feedback as if to hide any discomfort.[9] The result is a guitar leading the charge, screeching and dripping acid throughout the album like a rabid animal. This contrasts with their forthcoming albums, where Karoli plays much more of a supporting role in tandem with every other member so that no one is more important than anyone else.

After his therapist suggested that the music was not good for his mental health, Malcolm Mooney quit the band and returned to America; he would soon be replaced by Damo Suzuki. Born in Japan in 1950, Suzuki left at the age of eighteen and busked his way across Europe before ending up in Germany. In May of 1970, Holger Czukay and Jaki Liebezeit were in a café watching Suzuki. "He was somehow praying to the sun and making loud noises, singing or chanting. I turned to Jaki and said: 'This is our new singer,'" Czukay recalled to *Louder Sound*'s Rob Hughes.[10] Czukay and Liebezeit invited Suzuki to sing on stage with them that very night at the Blow Up Club. There was no rehearsal, just a baptism by fire, but Suzuki emerged triumphant. "And it worked out in a totally unexpected way. On stage he started out very calm and peaceful, then suddenly—like a Samurai warrior—he switched and became the exact opposite. The audience were frightened by him. It was like when the Sex Pistols first came out," Czukay said.[11]

Released in 1970, Can's next album, *Soundtracks*, is the only album in their discography containing contributions from both Mooney and Suzuki, as some of the songs were recorded before the former departed. As the name implies, the songs that comprise *Soundtracks* were composed for different films—Roland Klick's *Deadlock*, Leon Capetanos's *Cream–Schwabing Report*, Roger Fritz's *Mädchen mit Gewalt*, Jerzy Skolimowski's *Deep End*, and Thomas Schamoni's *Ein großer graublauer Vogel*—so that the band could secure additional income. This was at a time when it was more common for films to outsource their soundtracks from psychedelic bands, with Pink Floyd composing the score for Barbet Schroeder's film *More* the prior year. Despite being a clear transition, *Soundtracks* is still a worthy album that represents the band exploring beyond Velvet Underground-inspired psych. "Tango Whiskyman," featuring Damo Suzuki on vocals, has the eerie night dance ritual of some of their songs to come, while "She Brings the Rain" shows a genuine love for old jazz. Still, the main highlight is the longest song, the nearly fifteen-minute "Mother Sky," which unfolds like "Yoo Doo Right" but with more ebb and flow.

The Damo Suzuki Era

With Suzuki as a full member now, the band created their three most renowned albums, *Tago Mago*, *Ege Bamyasi*, and *Future*

Days, released over subsequent years between 1971 and 1973. It cannot be stressed enough that these three albums are unmistakably Can, but also fundamentally different from one another. Give *Tago Mago* to someone who wants to know how extreme rock music can be; give *Ege Bamyasi* to alternative or indie rock fans; give *Future Days* to listeners of ambient music, which it predates by a few years. Can's twists and turns during this period are reminiscent of Miles Davis's albums released across the ocean when he went fusion. Consider *Tago Mago* the krautrock version of *Bitches Brew* (chaotic double albums), consider *Ege Bamyasi* to be their version of *On the Corner* (twitchy funk-based albums), and consider *Future Days* to be their version of *In a Silent Way* (impossibly gorgeous summer night albums). These comparisons are strengthened by the fact that Miles Davis's producer Teo Macero spliced together takes in the same way Holger Czukay did for Can, using the studio as an instrument in a way that hadn't been used before in the world of jazz. Finally, it's worth mentioning that Miles Davis was inspired by Karlheinz Stockhausen during the making of *On the Corner*.

Like *Bitches Brew*, *Tago Mago* is a double album, and two of its sides are devoted to only one single track each: "Halleluwah" and "Aumgn." To that end, it dispenses any notion of normalcy early on. "Paperhouse" has a tentative start, but soon shifts into high gear with Jaki Liebezeit's insectoid, motorik clicking of drums, over which Karoli's guitar shreds and soars. "Mushroom" is the only song on *Tago Mago* that clocks in under five minutes, in which Suzuki shrieks against the atomic bomb that devastated his home country: "When I saw mushroom head / I was born and I was dead." Suzuki's way of singing is unique, akin to the Cocteau Twins' Liz Fraser or Michael Stipe on early R.E.M. records. One can picture him with his eyes closed while feeling out the groove of his bandmates, eventually opening his mouth and letting whatever sounds come out naturally, and if they should so happen to form words, all the better. To prove how the words themselves do not matter, "Oh Yeah" is a mix of backwards vocals, English lyrics, and then Japanese lyrics.

This is all crazy enough but it culminates in "Halleluwah," an eighteen-minute powerhouse that hip-hop fans might recognize because the piano bridge was sampled by A Tribe Called Quest on their comeback album. If "Halleluwah" is pure groove, then the following track, "Aumgn," should be considered anti-groove. It is, by far, the least approachable song that Can put on a studio album. At times, it sounds like a playground on fire set against a swarm of locusts. Running over seventeen minutes long, it is almost the equivalent length of "Halleluwah."

Buried underneath the preceding hour, "Peking O" contains a novel innovation by bringing in a drum machine. Writer Jan Reetze believes this to be the first German rock song to ever make use of this new technology, but whereas most bands would use a drum machine as the primary rhythmic device, Can use it as just another texture, a synthetic counterpart to the organic percussion from Liebezeit, adding to Can's mass of sound. (They would play with the drum machine again on the next album's "Spoon.") The drum machine's rhythm begins as a strange and cheap bossa nova before Liebezeit begins improvising with it, alternating between a breathless pummel and practically rhythmless bursts. Given these preceding songs, it was nice of Can to close the album with its most serene song, at least until the climax where Liebezeit lets loose on the drums. But for the first three minutes or so, "Bring Me Coffee or Tea" is exactly as the title suggests, a postdinner drink with a hint of sweetness, with Karoli's guitar and Holger's bass pinging gently along, creating a sort of "sonic rhyme" with another.

At seven tracks, *Ege Bamyasi* may have the same number of songs as *Tago Mago*, but that it runs thirty-three minutes shorter highlights the key difference: this is a collection of songs instead of a collection of side-long grooves and experiments. "Soup" is the most "out there" song of the album, yet it only runs to ten minutes—bite-sized compared to some of the songs on *Tago Mago*. Aside from "Soup," the album's only other long song is "Pinch" at nine minutes and a half, which sounds very much like Miles Davis's dense, funky *On the Corner*, released the month before.

More than Can's other albums, *Ege Bamyasi* has become famous through name-drops and samples from other artists. Pavement's Stephen Malkmus has been quoted as saying, "I played Can's *Ege Bamyasi* album every night before I went to sleep for about three years," before covering the album in full while on tour in Cologne.[12] Elsewhere, Kanye West notably sampled "Sing Swan Song" for "Drunk and Hot Girls" on his third album, *Graduation*, while Texas indie rock stalwarts Spoon named themselves after one of the songs on this album. And to prove just how songful the album was, "Spoon" was a surprise success for the band, selling over three hundred thousand copies and reaching number six on the German charts thanks to its use as the signature theme song for German TV thriller *Das Messer*.

Whereas *Monster Movie* and *Tago Mago* both had a paranoid, gothic darkness to them, *Ege Bamyasi* can be characterized by healthiness. Not only does the album promote a can of okra on the cover, but song titles that include "Vitamin C," "Soup," and "I'm So Green" seem to point to the importance of healthy eating—indeed, Suzuki gives one of his most passionate performances as he warns about losing your vitamin C. And, of course, the can of okra is not merely a cheeky reference to the band's name, but also references Andy Warhol's famous Campbell's soup can paintings, further strengthening the Velvet Underground connection.

The album that came after, *Future Days*, is even healthier: Suzuki's vocals sound more melodic than ever before; compared to *Tago Mago* and *Ege Bamyasi*, both of which had moments of Suzuki shouting and screaming over the din, there are no such songs here. More than their previous two albums, *Future Days* is purely textural: every instrument seems to waft in the mix, inviting you into its summery haze. Looking back, Suzuki says,

> *Future Days* is for me the best album I made with Can. Because it was very easy to quit from Can after that album. I wanted nothing from them after that. Musically I was very satisfied.... Nobody else arrived at such a space. It's just a new dimension. With that album I was really free, it was no longer necessary to make music after.[13]

Whereas both *Tago Mago* and *Ege Bamyasi* contain seven individual songs, *Future Days* returns to *Monster Movie*'s four-track setup, including one short one and one superlong one. The shortest one, "Moonshake," is in the model of the last few twitchy and groovy songs from *Ege Bamyasi*, and, despite its whimsical psychedelia, fits in among the rest of the album's quietude. Elsewhere, "Spray" nods at jazz fusion that had become the dominant form of jazz across the Atlantic and sounds very much like the humid, alien world explored on Herbie Hancock's *Sextant* released that same year. Meanwhile, one can only guess how many times Brian Eno had heard the title track and "Bel Air" when ambient music was still a twinkle in his ear. Unlike the previous assaults of *Monster Movie* or *Tago Mago*, both of those songs seem to subside into the background, whereupon they create their own little dream worlds for you to inhabit. Whereas once, on *Tago Mago*, Suzuki sang about "Driving my way back to yesterday," on *Future Days* he now looks ahead, cautiously yet optimistically: "It's all for the sake of future days."

After Suzuki

After *Future Days*, Damo Suzuki left the band to marry his girlfriend and join Jehovah's Witnesses for a time, leaving the band once more with no singer. *Soon over Babaluma* was released in 1974, featuring Karoli and Schmidt taking up vocal duties. Akin to Genesis' *A Trick of the Tail*, which followed original front man Peter Gabriel's departure and Phil Collins taking the reigns as the band's lead vocalist, Karoli and Schmidt do a fine job emulating Suzuki's style, such that the shaman-singer was not missed. At least not yet. "Dizzy Dizzy" and "Come Sta, La Luna" easily rank among the band's best songs. "Dizzy Dizzy" features Karoli playing violin like a country fiddle (Karoli had inherited his grandfather's Gypsy violin when he was seven years old, and it's a shame we don't get to hear him play violin more often on Can records). Meanwhile, "Come Sta, La Luna" is reminiscent of previous, slippery, evening ritual dance music like "Tango Whiskyman." The second half of the album leans harder into the previous album's atmosphere and jazz fusion, which may contribute to the disappointment. After reinventing themselves over and over, the band sound cautious for the first time, retreading old ground. But it should be of no surprise that a band renowned for its instrumentals and less so their vocals would be able to carry on without its main vocalist.

It was not until *Landed* the following year that the band that we knew as Can began to move away from what made them special. *Landed* has significantly more polish to it, making use of better technology as the band made the jump to sixteen-track recording, losing a lot of the mystery that shrouded their tracks before. Other than Czukay and Schmidt singing on "Full Moon on the Highway," Michael Karoli is responsible for lead vocals again, but he's singing far more than he was on *Soon over Babaluma*, exposing him as far less interesting a singer when he's not emulating Suzuki. Amon Düül II producer Olaf Kübler shows up on tenor saxophone on "Red Hot Indians," a rare instance of Can opening their "inner space" to an outsider, while "Unfinished" is reminiscent of the far more experimental tracks they used to make on *Tago Mago*, but it's ultimately not enough to recommend the album in full.

In the years that followed, Can became less of a rock band and even more of a groove band than they were before. Released in 1976, *Flow Motion* is the strongest of all the late-period Can albums. The rhythms are still fertile enough that the reggae-inspired "Laugh Till You Cry, Live Till You Die" and Moroccan-inspired fusion workout of "Smoke (E.F.S. No. 59)" both have blood flowing in them. The former was sparked when a visiting Brian Eno introduced Michael Karoli to Jamaican dub pioneer Lee "Scratch" Perry, marking one of the last studio songs in their career where the band tried something genuinely new. Meanwhile, "Smoke" is one of many numerated works that belongs to Can's Ethnological Forgery Series (E.F.S.), which was exclusively to explore different styles of different music around the world years before it was in vogue to do so. *Flow Motion* also contains the disco jam "I Want More," which nabbed Can their only British hit which led to an appearance on *Top of the Pops*. "I Want More" is infectiously catchy, made possible by having all members of Can sing the hook.

Traffic bassist Rosko Gee and percussionist Rebop Kwaku Baah joined the band afterwards. Only having become the band's bassist because there was no one else to take up the role, Holger Czukay felt that his playing was being outpaced by his bandmates at this time. To boot, he had double duties of playing bass and editing the tapes, and so he off-loaded bass playing to Rosko Gee, such that on their 1977 album, *Saw Delight*, Czukay is credited only for tape manipulation and sound effects. So perhaps it's no surprise that this would be his last album with Can before leaving to pursue his solo career. *Saw Delight*'s opener "Don't Say No" sounds suspiciously like *Future Days'* "Moonshake" with a less enticing vocal part, and the album doesn't get much better from there. Jaki Liebezeit, whose muscular forearms helped define and distinguish those early Can albums, has a significantly reduced role on these records, with his ridiculous fills and clicks replaced by Rebop Kwaku Baah on percussion.

Can released two more albums before they eventually called it quits: *Out of Reach* in 1978 and *Can* in 1979. The former is rightfully regarded as Can's worst album, and the band themselves have tried to distance themselves from it by choosing not to reissue it alongside their other albums until 2014. The latter is slightly better as there's more space in the mix, allowing both the grooves and Karoli's guitar to sing more. It also contains the ninety-ninth entry into Can's E.F.S. in "Can Can," which was released as the album's single, producing a fun if superfluous take on the cancan dance. Can could never resist a little humor, hence the punny titles and album covers of *Ege Bamyasi* (with its album art of a can) and *Saw Delight*.

As the '70s came to a close, Can had reached its natural end. Jaki Liebezeit compared the trajectory of a band to that of a dog or a marriage: "a group lives about as long as a dog. After ten years at the most, it's over. Like in a marriage. At some time the excitement wanes."[14] Thus, Can's best period was ultimately short-lived: Damo Suzuki was only a member for three and a half studio albums, while Mooney was only a member for one and a half, not counting the 1989 reunion album, *Rite Time,* which is marred by unfortunate '80s production and doesn't have the bite and bile of *Monster Movie.*

Extras, Live and Lost Tapes, and Solo Albums

Their discography doesn't end there, however. More than nearly any other band, the archival releases, live albums and bootlegs are part of the Can experience. For fans of *Monster Movie*, the 1991 compilation *Delay 1968* contains songs that were recorded in the early days with Mooney, and is essential listening. "Butterfly" contains insane chicken-scratch guitar, while Mooney's vocal on "Nineteen Century Man" is a fun James Brown impression. *Delay 1968* also contains the brooding "Thief," which was notably covered extensively by Radiohead on their *Hail to the Thief* tour.

In addition to *Delay 1968*, *Limited Edition* (released in 1974, and so named because it was originally a limited release and later reissued as *Unlimited Edition*) and *The Lost Tapes* (released in 2012) are both generous collections of outtakes, both of which feature songs with Mooney and Suzuki. Releases such as these paint a picture of an alternate universe where Can fans would have received two or even three full studio albums with Mooney before he was replaced by Suzuki. Both *Limited Edition* and *The Lost Tapes* also contain curiosities, answering questions like "what if Jaki Liebezeit played trumpet?" ("E.F.S. No. 36"), "what if you're waiting for the streetcar was akin to *Waiting for Godot*?" ("Waiting for the Streetcar"), and "what if Can tried their hand at early American blues?" ("The Loop").

Whereas their studio albums would have used tape manipulation to achieve the perfect song, the bootlegs and live shows tell a different story, one of pure physical prowess; this is why live albums of the band are still sought after to this day. For example, *Live in Stuttgart 1975* and *Live in Brighton 1975* were both released by Mute in 2021, and both present a differing snapshot of where Can was in 1975 than their studio album from that year, *Landed*, which is barely represented across these two shows. Instead, the band builds new grooves from the ground up, or deconstructs old classics and gives them new names (the immortal bassline and organ melody on "Vitamin C" are slowed down on *Brighton 1975*'s "Sieben," akin to Sly & the Family Stone's dirgy version of "Thank You (Falettinme Be Mice Elf Agin)" that closed out *There's a Riot Goin' On*).

Can's individual members never stopped making music outside of the group either. Irmin Schmidt scored films and television shows and returned to his classical roots. Holger Czukay released his debut solo album *Movies* in 1979 shortly after he left the band, and considers it to be "the logical continuation of [his] work with Can's last years of active existence."[15] The album is loaded with television and radio samples, years before the technique had become embedded in the hip-hop and electronic genres, while also predating Brian Eno and David Byrne's *My Life in the Bush of Ghosts* on that front by two years. These samples are placed over instruments played by and large by Czukay himself, although some Can members lend a helping hand: Rebop Kwaku Baah plays the chicken organ on "Cool in the Pool," Schmidt and Karoli play piano and guitar respectively on "Oh Lord Give Us More Money," and Jaki Liebezeit plays drums throughout. For anyone puzzled about why Can struck gold on "I Want More" and then never capitalized on a similar sounding track again, Czukay gives us "Cool in the Pool," using a very similar whispered hook.

After *Movies* came 1982's *Full Circle*, credited to Czukay, Liebezeit, and former Public Image Ltd bassist Jah Wobble. *Full Circle* isn't krautrock at all but rather a dub record released in the same year that also saw titanic releases in the genre like Horace Andy's *Dance Hall Style*, Wayne Jarrett's *Showcase Vol. 1*, and Scientist's *Scientist Wins the World*. Dub is a form of reggae that makes heavy use of studio techniques to make the drums feel heavy and atmospheric, and where Can once tried their hand on reggae on *Flow Motion*, dub feels more natural here thanks to Holger Czukay's editing and overdubbing prowess. Similar to *Movies* and his sophomore album *On the Way to the Peak of Normal*, Czukay handles the bulk of the instruments, although he gives bass duties to Jah Wobble. "How Much Are They?" has a very heavy, stomping bass from Wobble, bursts of French horn from Czukay, and very dubby drums in the song's climax, but the most exciting section is the piano breakdown near the middle.

A few years later, Holger and Liebezeit would collaborate with David Sylvian of the band Japan, when Sylvian himself went ambient on the albums *Plight + Premonition* and *Flux + Mutability*, while Liebezeit would go on to work with Faust's keyboardist Hans Joachim Irmler on the album *Flut*. Damo Suzuki eventually left the Jehovah's Witnesses and returned to music, forming the Damo Suzuki Band in 1986 with Jaki Liebezeit. The Damo Suzuki Band were predominantly a live act, but they eventually released one studio album in 1998, *Vernissage*, that unfortunately fails to capture the same mysterious atmosphere of the Can records that Suzuki was a part of. Suzuki currently leads the Damo Suzuki Network, where he performs live improvisations with local musicians. Between the numerous side projects that the Can men were involved with and unearthed live shows that are being released decades later, I'm reminded of how "Yoo Doo Right," the twenty-minute behemoth of Can's debut album, was pulled from a six-hour studio jam: the studio albums only provide glimpses of a motorik groove that's still pounding years later.

2 The German Beatles: Faust

Origins

Faust is rightfully regarded as one of krautrock's most notable bands, but if krautrock is defined by its motorik beat, then Faust presents a paradox, because they are anti-motorik. Actually, they were anti-everything: anti-label, anti-song, anti-expectations. They were positioned to their label as what could be the German version of the Beatles even though they didn't have a song in them, much less a hit. They became a cult band outside their home country because of a collection of B-sides. Faust was the antithesis of the rhythm behind bands like Can and Neu!: instead of a deliberate beat that signaled a band on the move, Faust would deliberately interrupt the beat with their collage approach and often not even bother with a beat.

Those methods, combined with their notorious live antics, where they treated the stage the same as a recording studio, sometimes showing up to watch TV naked or playing pinball, might make them seem like a novelty act.[1] But Faust never cared about other people's opinions and certainly not that of their label heads. "We didn't care about conventions and we were not looking for stardom," bassist Jean-Hervé Péron said in an interview with *The Guardian*. "We were looking for our own music, and when I say our own I mean European, more specifically German—a music that would express all the needs and worries and dreams of German youth at the time."[2] That is no more evident than in the name they chose for themselves, taken from Johann Wolfgang von Goethe's legendary play, considered by some the single most important work of German literature, while simultaneously being the German word for "fist" to symbolize the musical revolution that they were part of.[3]

Like other krautrock groups, Faust's music was ultimately a reaction to postwar German culture. In an interview with *The Guardian*, keyboardist Hans Joachim Irmler made as much clear:

> Hitler destroyed music ... It was forbidden to play this and that, so after the breakdown of the Third Reich, there was nothing left to build on except the very fantastic English and American musicians. We thought, "Let the British do what they are able to do, because they are brilliant, but we don't have to make the same—that's bullshit." I can't see why I should try to play like Cream or whatever. So Faust is a unique idea, because we didn't want to follow the common music ideas.[4]

So whereas Amon Düül II, Can, and Embryo were looking at American music for inspiration, Faust was on a quest of pure self-invention, of what it meant to be a German band. And the way they did that was by eradicating any trace of blues, jazz, or funk—of American music—from their version of rock.

The Original Run

Famously, the record label Polydor asked journalist Uwe Nettelbeck for a band that could become the German equivalent of the Beatles. Absurd now as it may seem, Nettelbeck presented them with Faust. This worked because Nettelbeck had pull as an important counterculture writer, while Faust's founding organist Hans Joachim Irmler recalled that everyone at the label cared more about the business side over music, and they were able to pull the wool over their eyes by convincing them that they could be the next pop music phenomenon even though they had no intention of being such a thing.[5] If Faust were the Beatles, they were the Beatles of "Revolution #9." To help develop what was supposed to be a huge hitmaker, Polydor gave Faust 30,000 deutsch marks (approximately 60,000 euros today), an unheard of amount of money for an experimental group to acquire, much of which was likely lost in copious drug consumption.[6]

In addition to Irmler, Faust was comprised of bassist Jean-Hervé Péron, guitarist-keyboardist Rudolf Sosna, drummers Werner "Zappi" Diermaier and Arnulf Meifert, and saxophonist Gunther Wüsthoff. Polydor also financed a newly built studio in the rural village of Wümme where Faust moved to, mirroring the retreat of many krautrock bands out of the big cities. Left to their own devices, Faust recorded their 1971 debut album, *Faust*, in one night.

Opener "Why Don't You Eat Carrots" begins with what may as well have been Faust's mission statement, briefly sampling the Rolling Stones'"(I Can't Get No) Satisfaction" and the Beatles' "All You Need Is Love," only for those recognizable sounds to disintegrate into Rudolf Sosna's heavily distorted slide guitar, as if to say, "enough of those bands. Here's us now." Though the album is only thirty-five minutes long, Faust does not make it easy for listeners. There are only three tracks, and each song is protracted with no apparent structure. A guitar solo on "Meadow Meal" is suddenly interrupted by a sudden slab of noise, while the sound of would-be tranquil rain later on in that same song is offset by a high-pitched drone. Taking up the entire second side on its own, "Miss Fortune" is the longest of the three tracks, consisting of bird squawks, distorted laughter, piano peeking in and out, and a disembodied voice going on and on about who-knows-what.

There are other strange and cacophonous albums in krautrock, but Faust's debut stands out as the craziest. They never cared to be professional musicians, preferring a Dadaist approach of expressing total, uninhibited nonsense. And of course, no other band had the same circumstances of Faust, a group of misfits that landed on a windfall of label money and freedom.

Equally striking to the music was the physical packaging of *Faust*, which remains unique. The vinyl itself was transparent, something that the band had to fight with the manufacturers to produce because the manufacturers were worried that it would impact the quality of the music.[7] To add to that, the sleeve and insert are also both transparent, while the only art is an X-ray image of a closed fist in reference to their name and musical revolution.

After their debut, Meifert was given the boot, and Diermaier took on the role as the band's sole drummer. According to Jean-Hervé Péron, reasons cited for Meifert's removal included "because he had flat buttocks and an absolutely beautiful girlfriend," but most of all, because Meifert was a straight shooter: "because he practiced everyday, because he always kept his room neat and woke up every morning to first wet a cloth he'd put in front of his room to keep the dirt out, because he played such a hard 4/4th," and thus, did not fit into the band's anarchist philosophy and approach to music.[8]

Predictably, Faust's debut did not sell well—only a measly thousand copies despite the money Polydor invested in it. Their complete lack of commerciality was compounded by their unorthodox live performances at the time: their first gig in Hamburg had each member armed with a black box giving them the ability to turn down another member's volume if they didn't like what was being played, like their own trollish version of John Cage's indeterminacy. Naturally, Polydor was not pleased. "[T]hey put pressure on us to make more 'accessible' music. It was for us an interesting experiment to try and make 'normal' music," Péron said in an interview with *It's Psychedelic Baby Magazine*.[9] "In the end it turned out to be bizarre music anyway."

"It's a Rainy Day, Sunshine Girl," the opener of their second album, 1972's *Faust So Far*, loops a thudding, dry backbeat to the point of pure annoyance. Tellingly, the seven-minute song contains no verse, chorus, or bridge. Instead, the lyrics are merely the title's words repeated until it's turned into a sort of Dada mantra. Meanwhile, the repetitive beat of "It's a Rainy Day, Sunshine Girl" represents Faust's resilience: it didn't matter that Polydor would soon drop them, they would simply continue to be Faust some other way. Whereas each song on *Faust* was long, the songs on *Faust So Far* are much shorter, including five songs that are tiny little fragments that would have been strung together into a single collage had it still been 1971, including a surprisingly pretty folk song in "On the Way to Adamae." Aside from "It's a Rainy Day, Sunshine Girl," the album's other highlight is "No Harm," which similarly repeats one nonsense phrase over and over: "Daddy, take a banana. Tomorrow is Sunday!"

Shorter songs or not, *So Far* didn't sell either, and so Polydor promptly dropped Faust. But the band got another lucky break when then-head of Virgin Records, Richard Branson, signed them and released their third album, *The Faust Tapes*, in 1973. *The Faust Tapes* was part of a marketing scheme Virgin devised where full albums were released for the price of a single, enticing audiences to hear an entire album for forty-eight pence. It worked for Faust: Virgin was able to move sixty thousand sales of the album in Britain that year, even though they lost the equivalent of 2,000 pounds sterling while doing so.[10] Unfortunately, the low price made *The Faust Tapes* ineligible for chart placement.[11] Yet because of this devious tactic, Faust would be emblematic of so many krautrock bands: virtually unknown in their home country of Germany, they managed to break into the UK market.

UK listeners wouldn't have heard anything as striking as *Faust* nor as strange but at least tuneful as "It's a Rainy Day, Sunshine Girl." Instead, *The Faust Tapes* is a collection of experiments and demos, obscured by the fact that the original pressing contained no titles and presented each side as one track apiece, such that the album plays like a collage of ideas. Despite the album's half-baked nature, some songs are worthy enough to seek it out. "Flashback Caruso" plays like a bucolic folk song, accidentally aligning it with some of the British prog bands at this time, and ends with gorgeous piano chords. Meanwhile, "J'ai Mal Aux Dents" rattles around incessantly, befitting the title (French for "I Have a Toothache"). The success of *The Faust Tapes* allowed Faust to tour the UK, where they famously mixed music with industrial tools like jackhammers on stage, a stunt that would later inspire acts like German industrial group Einstürzende Neubauten.

The year 1973 also saw the release of their collaborative album with Tony Conrad, a New York filmmaker and member of the Theatre of Eternal Music, sometimes referred to as the Dream Syndicate, which also included notable members of the New York avant-garde like La Monte Young (one of the great minimalist composers) and John Cale (before Cale was part of the Velvet Underground). Fittingly then, this album with Faust would be titled *Outside the Dream Syndicate*. Conrad was in Europe at the time working with La Monte Young, and was introduced to Uwe Nettelbeck. As Conrad was poor at the time, he welcomed any opportunity to be in a recording studio again. "At the time I couldn't afford a studio any more than a Mercedes. I was poor as could be. When they offered a studio, I was really excited, and I didn't really care about the idea of releasing a vinyl at that time because I thought secretly that they'd never do it because my music is too far out," he said in an interview with *The Quietus*.[12]

Outside the Dream Syndicate is composed only of two songs, one on each side. Both tracks more closely resemble the American minimalists, specifically La Monte Young, than anything that Can had done. Whereas Can brought the implied beat of minimalism to the fore and turned it into rock music, Conrad and Faust de-emphasized the rock component. Opener "From the Side of Man and Womankind" features only a simple drum beat from Werner Diermaier and a single note on guitar. According to Conrad, "Faust wasn't so happy with this thing because they really wanted to rock out, so we did another track with synthesizer and everything, and that filled up the whole tape that was in the budget."[13] The result was the B-side "From the Side of the Machine," but "rock out" is misleading even if Jean-Hervé Péron does play bass and the drums are far more active: Conrad's drone is the most engaging element yet again.

Outside the Dream Syndicate was buried. "It got slammed with a couple of small reviews in the press that said it was totally uncommercial, and that was the end of it. It showed up in a few cut out bins here and there," Conrad recalled, even though he loved the album.[14] It wasn't until two decades later that more people got the chance to hear it when a newly created American label, Table of the Elements, gave the album a long overdue CD reissue in 1993.

Anyone in the UK who purchased *The Faust Tapes* and wasn't immediately turned off by the experimental nature of its songs would have been impressed to follow Faust through their next album and magnum opus, *Faust IV*, which was recorded at Richard Branson's Manor Studio in the English village of Shipton-on-Cherwell at the same time that Mike Oldfield was recording *Tubular Bells*. The twelve-minute opener, "Krautrock," can be taken as Faust poking fun at their contemporaries like Neu! who droned for lengthy periods of time over the same one or two chords. Except, parody or not, "Krautrock" turns out masterfully.

Similar to *Faust So Far*, the album is split between longer songs and shorter songs, almost alternating between these two modes. Venturing into satire, "The Sad Skinhead" features a skinhead's lament on a previous relationship over a reggae pastiche: "I always felt good with you / Going places, smashing faces." "Jennifer" and "It's a Bit of a Pain" show a rare tender side to Faust; the former even sounds strangely romantic for a band so thoroughly uninvested in love, while the latter might have been modeled after the quiet third Velvet Underground album if it weren't for the intrusive electronic noises. They didn't want to be seen as too tender, after all.

Faust IV would be the last Faust album for some time. Péron put it simplest: "Same procedure as with Polydor. Richard Branson wanted us to be popular and we did not," and so they were dropped from Virgin.[15] This time, they did not survive. Still pretending to be a hot product from Virgin, they racked up an exorbitant bill at a hotel and were thrown in prison when they tried to escape rather than paying the 30,000 deutsch marks.[16] Instead of hopping to another label, Faust disappeared.

Comeback

In 1990, Irmler, Diermaier, and Péron reunited for some performances, but they would not release a new product until 1994. That would end up as a big year for Faust, marking their first tour in the United States (even if it was only Diermaier and Péron) with members of Sonic Youth opening for them, and the release of their first official album in two decades.[17] *Rien* was released in 1994 via Table of the Elements, and, according to the back cover, was mixed and produced by Jim O'Rourke, soon to be known for his work behind the boards for artists such as Sonic Youth, Wilco, and Joanna Newsom, to say nothing of his own solo career.

"Mixed and produced" is putting it lightly. According to Jim O'Rourke, he is responsible for the entirety of the album's creation. The title tells the joke (also declared aloud on the first song): there is "Rien de Faust" ("Nothing of Faust" in French) on it. O'Rourke said in an interview in *Frequency*, "[Faust] had nothing to do with the record. The whole thing is a tape collage. There is nothing on there that is actually played." Instead, O'Rourke built the entire album from scratch using recordings of Faust's live shows as tracing paper:

> I went through them and found a point where the bass drum was hit and you can't hear anything else, so that's my bass drum. And oh, here's a guitar part where he plays a note very distinctly and you can't hear anything else. So, all of the guitar

parts and the singing and everything else is all pieced together note by note.[18]

That certainly explains why *Rien* doesn't sound anything like the classic Faust of the 1970s beyond the drone-and-simple-drum of "Listen to the Fish." The second, untitled song is the best of the bunch, sounding cacophonous and demonstrating their kinship to industrial rock. Unfortunately, midway through, a twitchy drum pattern emerges and feels like it's building toward some incredible climax only to suddenly jolt to a halt, as if O'Rourke ran out of material to continue. Thus, the following album, *You Know Faust*, feels like a conscious course-correction to sound more like classic Faust, straight down to a two-minute folk instrumental interlude in "Cendre" recalling the quiet songs of their third and fourth albums.

Faust would put out many other records afterwards, including 2004's *Derbe Respect, Alder*, a collaborative release with New Jersey experimental hip-hop group Dälek, and *Outside the Dream Syndicate: Alive*, a live album with Tony Conrad and Jim O'Rourke recorded in 1995 and released in 2005, considered a sequel to Conrad and Faust's previous collaboration.[19]

In 2010 came *Faust Is Last*, whose album cover was a deliberate nod to their debut album almost forty years before. Made up of twenty-two individual tracks, *Faust Is Last* goes down much easier than many of their previous albums, even though a lot of it is noisy industrial rock. There are occasional moments of respite, such as the piano ballad "Day Out," that closes out the first disc, but for the most part, these are far less interesting than the rock songs where Kraan drummer Jan Fride Wolbrandt bashes out his kit as if he were in a garage rock band. "I Don't Buy Your Shit No More" sounds like so much of the punk and indie rock that krautrock had a hand in influencing in the first place. There is a finality in the title *Faust Is Last* that suggested it might be their last album, and in a manner of speaking it was: it was the last Faust album to include original founder Hans Joachim Irmler, although Jean-Hervé Péron and Werner Diermaier have kept the band alive.

3 Out of the City and into the Forst: Cluster and Harmonia

Origins

In isolated farmhouses in the rural village of Forst, West Germany, two musicians named Dieter Moebius and Hans-Joachim Roedelius—known together as Cluster, and as Harmonia when joined by Neu!'s Michael Rother—would create some of the most influential German music of the '70s: ambient and electronic music made within the context of krautrock. Later on, British musician and producer Brian Eno would visit them in Forst, collaborating and living with them in their mini-commune, and giving them a larger audience outside Germany.

Cluster's story began under a different name: Kluster. In 1968 musicians Conrad Schnitzler, Hans-Joachim Roedelius, and Boris Schaak co-founded the Zodiac Free Arts Lab, a venue that was a lightning rod for Berlin's experimental music scene, including German free jazz titan Peter Brötzmann and a band of teenagers named Agitation Free who played as the venue's house band.[1] The Zodiac Free Arts Lab was unfortunately short-lived, shutting down in 1969 after only a few months of being active after Schnitzler lost interest in running it. It certainly did not help that the club was the frequent target of police raids because of the prevalent drug use of its clientele.

Born in 1934, Hans-Joachim Roedelius was originally a child actor during the Nazi Germany era, having starred in films including 1938's *Verklungene Melodie*.[2] After the war, Roedelius managed to leave East Berlin for West Berlin, where he worked a number of odd jobs, including as a nurse and masseur. It was in West Berlin, where, already an adult, Roedelius developed a fascination with avant-garde music despite no musical training.[3]

By contrast, his bandmate Conrad Schnitzler came from a musical background. But although his father was a trained musician, Schnitzler wanted no part in it. "All these people making music with the drums and flutes, I hated it—and melodies that were like worms in your head. All day long, rattling in your head," Schnitzler remembered in an interview with *Red Bull Music Academy*. "Only if you can't play instruments can you really make free sounds. And I wanted to have noise/ sounds composed together—a steam hammer here, a bird piping there, a car goes by... and be like the director of all this. As an artist, you have to create something new."[4]

Born in Switzerland in 1944, Dieter Moebius moved to West Berlin to study art, eventually befriending Schnitzler and Roedelius. Together, they formed the noise trio Kluster after the Zodiac Free Arts Lab closed down. The music made by the trio across their three albums—*Klopfzeichen* (1970), *Zwei-Osterei* (1971), and *Eruption* (recorded in 1971, released in 1996)—is thoroughly uncompromising. Had they been released in England a few years later, people could mistake them for the industrial works of Throbbing Gristle. Each of these albums are dark masses of pure sound, and while sometimes instruments can be picked out—the drum pulse of *Klopfzeichen*, or the sawing cello of *Zwei-Osterei*—they are, for the most part, acts of glorious noise with little regard for the safety of listeners.

Listening to Kluster, you might think that the primary influence was the avant-garde composers of Europe, such as Karlheinz Stockhausen, but that was not the case according to Hans-Joachim Roedelius: "Our biggest influence was ourselves, our lives and the way we were appreciate living, not really other musicians. We can't count names, we listened to many people, of course. I listened to Pierre Henry and Iannis Xenakis at the time, just to know about them, not to copy them or do something that they did."[5] They also joked that they were trying to imitate the Velvet Underground in the same interview.

Kluster's second album, *Zwei-Osterei*, contains spoken religious text that was added because the album was, believe it or not, sponsored by the Catholic Church; although Schnitzler—I'm told—would prefer it if you did not understand the German words. The idea came from a Church cantor who "listened to one of our concerts in a basement in Düsseldorf somewhere, and said that it would be great to put text over it from the ecumenical movement," Roedelius said.[6] As the group wanted to put out an album without having to deal with a record company, they agreed to add the vocals afterwards.

Kluster was short-lived, with Schnitzler exiting to pursue a solo career, leaving the remaining members, Moebius and Roedelius, to make a small change to their name from Kluster to Cluster and start anew. Though Cluster would soon crystallize as a duo, their self-titled debut album briefly replaces Schnitzler with Conny Plank, who is credited both as a band member and producer.[7] Like the Kluster albums, there is nothing to hold on to: organs, Hawaiian guitars, and cellos are buried under effects and audio generators such that any organic instruments no longer sound natural. *Cluster* is only three tracks in length, but it is still a revelation compared to the two-track albums made by Kluster. By their second album, *Cluster II*, some structure and sounds begin coming into focus, even though the album is still intense in its noise and disregard for concepts such as melody. Some of the tones on *Cluster II* are genuinely scary, including the trippy organ of "Georgel" or the haunted house piano chords on "Nabitte" that make it feel like something is watching you.

Cluster made the move to leave West Berlin while the city was still isolated from the Iron Curtain, relocating to the rural Forst in Lower Saxony, West Germany.[8] Being surrounded by nature had a profound effect on Moebius and Roedelius, whose music abruptly shifted from noise to beauty, and from intensity to tranquility.

They were not the only German musicians that were leaving city life: Neu!'s Michael Rother (who was also an early member of Kraftwerk) left Düsseldorf in 1973 to join Cluster in their communal space in Forst, where the three formed the krautrock supergroup Harmonia, recording a trilogy of albums that rivals that of Rother's other group Neu!

Harmonia

Harmonia's legacy and sound is easy to summarize, a mixture of the soon-to-be starry keyboard melodies of Cluster and the earthbound pulse of Neu!, creating a sound that was as pastoral as it was modern. Their debut album, *Musik von Harmonia*, was self-produced and released in 1974 via Brain records. The album cover, designed by Rother, is reminiscent of the original intent behind the name Neu!: advertising. Here, the album cover was in the pop art style of the Düsseldorf bands Neu!

and Kraftwerk, depicting an advertisement for cleaning detergent, possibly referencing Rother's clean slate outside of Neu!, and Moebius's and Roedelius's clean slates outside of Cluster. That said, the album doesn't unify the three musicians' individual visions quite yet. For example, "Sonnenschein" and "Dino" are both short and chuggy and reminiscent of what Rother was doing with Neu!'s Klaus Dinger, just with more keyboards. That said, it is still an incredible debut. Opener "Watussi" is a highly melodic offering that looks forward to Cluster's *Zeiterzeit*. Meanwhile, "Sehr Kosmisch" makes use of warm keyboards and electronic drums, sounding like the inspiration point for so much dub and ambient house to come.

Their second album, *Deluxe*, released the following year, is a refinement on every front. There is less filler, the songs are more varied, and the mood is far warmer and more pastoral, leaning harder into the gold they struck on "Sehr Kosmisch." The record's warmth is thanks in no small part to the addition of Conny Plank as producer. "Deluxe (Immer Wieder)" features some chanted vocals, aligning Rother with what his original band Kraftwerk was doing without him. "Walky-Talky" is Harmonia's finest achievement, featuring Guru Guru drummer Mani Neumeier nudging the spacey loops along. "Monza (Rauf and Runter)" is a rousing seven-minute track that seeks to outdo Klaus Dinger's rock dream on *Neu! '75*. The organ on "Notre Dame" has a heady rush reminiscent of early Philip Glass.

That would have been the end of Harmonia. Moebius recalled later that *Musik von Harmonia* felt more like a Cluster album, whereas *Deluxe* felt more like Michael Rother's baby, and so they were happy not to continue with Harmonia anymore.[9] But that changed when Brian Eno visited Germany, en route to help David Bowie record *Low*, and asked to record with them.

By that point, Brian Eno's credentials included his tenure as part of the artsy glam group Roxy Music; he would soon embark on a uniquely quirky solo career and become, among other things, father of ambient music, founder of the Obscure label, and producer extraordinaire for acts that include Talking Heads, U2, and Coldplay. Eno was always musically curious, and immediately liked Harmonica when he visited Germany in 1974, even performing with them on stage in Hamburg before joining them in their little commune in Forst.[10]

Originally recorded in 1976, but not released until 1997 because the tapes were thought to be lost, *Tracks & Traces* is the result of Eno's studio collaboration with Harmonia. With Eno on board, they lean more into the ambient tracks of Harmonia's preceding albums and don't bother with the harder-edged tracks. The tracks also feature a previously unexplored sense of song structure, including shorter song lengths and Eno's own singing on "Luneburg Heath." Recorded in 1976, opener "Welcome" is clearly the basis for Eno's masterful "An Ending (Ascent)" from his 1983 ambient album, *Apollo: Atmospheres and Soundtracks.* Similarly, the title "By the Riverside" bears resemblance to Eno's "By the River," a song off 1977's *Before and after Science* that was co-written and performed with Moebius and Roedelius. "Atmosphere" is genuinely eerie in how the now-quartet treat the lone repeating keyboard chord, while "Les Demoiselles," sporting some gorgeous tones that resemble pedal steel guitars, has a happy bounce to it that can even be described as cute.

Sugar Time

After the release of *Musik von Harmonia*, Michael Rother left to fulfill his contractual obligation with Klaus Dinger as Neu!, and

Moebius and Roedelius worked on the next Cluster album, *Zuckerzeit*. *Zuckerzeit* credits Michael Rother on production, but that is misleading: Rother merely left behind his instruments for Moebius and Roedelius to use.[11] Not only is *Zuckerzeit* a radical departure from the noisy, less structured first two Cluster albums, but the album is also a departure in terms of how the duo created it. Rather than work together, each track is a solo composition, and the album is set up to alternate between the two composers all the way through. This way, it is also more evident to see the different approaches and philosophies of the two artists involved. Roedelius's "Hollywood" and "Marzipan" are sweetly melodic, appropriate for an album title that translates to "Sugar Time." Meanwhile, Moebius's songs like "Caramel" and "Rotor" tend to be fussier in drum programming, while his "James" feels like a glimpse into the inside of a squeaky-clean robot facility.

Zuckerzeit was already unclassifiable as rock music, but their following album, *Sowiesoso*, has even less claim. There's now zero heft in the percussion, coming away with one of the most alarmingly tender albums from Germany at this time. It reminds me of Can's *Future Days* in that regard, where a once-noisy and chaotic band paints an aural world of summer birds and blue skies for you to wander in. Whereas *Zuckerzeit* felt like a series of vignettes composed by two different people, *Sowiesoso* sounds like the unified vision of one single entity. The beatless coda of "Dem Wanderer," unrelated to the rest of the song, predicts the many pieces that Boards of Canada would add onto their longer songs on the IDM classic *Music Has the Right to Children*, while songs like "Sowiesoso" and "Es War Einmal" feel akin in spirit and color to Brian Eno's *Another Green World*—shorten and shuffle them into Eno's album and it would be hard to distinguish who made what, making it unsurprising that they would soon collaborate on two more albums.

By 1977, Eno had already dove into ambient music with the release of 1975's *Discreet Music*. The story of Eno's serendipitous "discovery" of ambient music is well-traveled: bedridden after an automobile accident, a friend visited him and brought him a record of eighteenth-century harp music. As Eno tells it,

> Having laid down, I realized that the amplifier was set at an extremely low level, and that one channel of the stereo had failed completely. Since I hadn't the energy to get up and improve matters, the record played on almost inaudibly. This presented what was for me a new way of hearing music—as part of the ambience of the environment just as the color of the light and the sound of the rain were parts of that ambience.[12]

Eno collaborated again with Cluster on 1977's *Cluster & Eno* and 1978's *After the Heat*, both released under the newly minted Sky Records, launched by Brain co-founder Günter Körber in 1975. The presence of Cluster on *Cluster & Eno* ensures that while the album may be regarded as an early ambient record, the album should not be treated as a link between *Discreet Music* or 1978's *Ambient 1: Music for Airports*. "Schöne Hände" has a mechanical whirr obscuring the song's gentle bass and keyboard, different than anything that Eno would have done alone. Furthermore, whereas the longer songs on Eno's solo ambient albums spanned sixteen to thirty minutes, the longest song on *Cluster & Eno* is only six minutes. The compositions are decidedly "bite-sized," reminiscent of Eno's work with Harmonia that had yet to be released by this point. Can bassist Holger Czukay contributes on opener "Ho Renomo," the only song here foreshadowing the widescreen ambient songs that Eno would soon make.

A mid-album highlight is "One," whose humid sitar drone makes it totally unlike anything Brian Eno had done in the 1970s, and as it turns out, Eno had nothing to do with it as Eno had to leave midway through recording. When there wasn't enough material for a full album, Cluster brought in guest musicians Asmus Tietchens and Okko Bekker, who largely produce the strangely spiritual "One," a title that may very well be a reference to the musician that doesn't appear in it: spell it backwards and see who's missing.

After the Heat came the year after. Instead of Cluster and Eno, the album is attributed to each musician separately—Eno & Moebius & Roedelius—likely because Hans-Joachim Roedelius launched his solo career that same year with the release of *Durch die Wüste*. That the order of their names on the title is flipped, with Eno now first on the billing, is revealing, as is the fact that almost all of the song titles are now in English. It feels like Eno has the greater role of the musicians, as some songs get downright weird, channeling the artsy songs that Eno was making in his solo career, such as the slow-moving funk dirge of "Broken Head" and the backwards vocals throughout "Tzima N'Arki," which again features bass from Holger Czukay.

Solo

Hans-Joachim Roedelius's solo career has been long and winding, with the releases under his own name numbering close to a hundred. Recorded in 1976 and released on Sky in 1978, his debut album, *Durch die Wüste*, contains "Am

Rockzipfel," a track far different than any of his work with Cluster that alternates between squelchy rock and wide-open ambient expanse, as if they were two sides to the same coin. "Regenmacher," a fascinating song of toy percussion from both Roedelius and Conny Plank, plus synthesizer from Moebius, is reminiscent of Cluster's brief post-Rother and pre-Eno *Zuckerzeit* era. Meanwhile, the *Selbstportraits* trilogy is composed of minimal organ pieces that Roedelius had recorded during the Cluster years.

Moebius would follow suit with his own solo career soon after. In contrast to Roedelius, Moebius's best solo albums sound decidedly nothing like Cluster, nor are they solo albums. Whereas Roedelius worked primarily on his own, Moebius continued to work with other musicians as if looking for a bond as strong as the one he shared with Roedelius, producing many collaborative albums with Gerd Beerbohm, Karl Renziehausen, Conny Plank (credited on the billing and not "merely" as a producer or session musician), and Guru Guru drummer Mani Neumeier.

Of note is *Material*, released under Moebius & Plank in 1981, and *Zero Set*, again with Plank but Neumeier as well, released in 1983. *Material* avoids easy categorization, but then again, so does all of krautrock. Opener "Conditioner" could have been friends with punk and new wave, and the way the chords bump into one another in the intro is reminiscent of the Ramones, except no melody is added on top. Instead, squelchy, squealing tones bounce along with the chords, creating an effect that is equal parts annoying and endearing. Meanwhile, "Tollkühn" and the majority of *Zero Set* look ahead to various forms of techno: the maddeningly catchy "All Repro" feels like something Aphex Twin might have made in the mid-'90s.

Over the years Roedelius and Moebius continued to reconnect and make music together as Cluster, but the Cluster albums trickled down slower and slower. Following 1978's *After the Heat*, the duo would release five more studio albums together: *Grosses Wasser* (1979), *Curiosum* (1981), *Apropos Cluster* (1990), *One Hour* (1994), and *Qua* (2015), none of which are as good as *Zuckerzeit* or *Sowiesoso*. *Grosses Wasser*, for example, sounds directionless following several years of perfecting ambient electronic music. But these final entries in their discography ultimately do not matter: Cluster's legacy had already been long solidified as a daring avant-garde noise group that effortlessly transitioned into proto-ambient melody makers, proving just what two musicians could do with only a few tools at their disposal in rural Germany. Create entire worlds, it turns out.

4 Marmalade Skies: Tangerine Dream

The Moog Synthesizer

It is impossible to talk about krautrock without eventually discussing the closely related "Berlin School" genre that came into prominence around the same time—in Berlin, of course— and shared the same social context but not the same sound. The term "Berlin School" is interchangeable with the German term *kosmische musik*, which translates to "cosmic music," bringing to mind the psychedelic subgenre of space rock made by bands like UFO and Hawkwind. Except the Berliners removed the rock component almost entirely when they embraced the synthesizer.

American engineer Robert Arthur Moog invented the Moog synthesizer in the mid-1960s, but the early adopters of the new instrument were mostly experimental composers, which he joked was "not what you'd call the basis for a big business" in an interview with *The Guardian*.[1] It would not be until near the end of the decade when his invention took off thanks to Wendy Carlos's 1968 album *Switched-On Bach*, which demonstrated the use of a synthesizer as more than just a sound effect machine or noise generator.

Switched-On Bach is, as the title suggests, a collection of pieces from German composer Johann Sebastian Bach performed on a Moog instead of a piano or harpsichord. Thus, the album had a novelty element and was an incredible success, eventually winning three Grammy awards and selling over a million copies, both rare feats for a classical album. But its biggest legacy is that it inspired musicians afterwards to get their hands on a Moog and try it for themselves.

While still in the Beatles, George Harrison released an experimental Moog solo album titled *Electronic Sound* in 1969. A few months later, the Moog would find its way on to a few tracks on the Beatles' *Abbey Road*, while Keith Emerson plays one on the self-titled debut album of Emerson, Lake, and Palmer released in 1970. And in the history of rock musicians toying around with the Moog synthesizer, I'd be remiss if I did not mention the Byrds' strange and psychedelic *Notorious Byrds Brothers*, one of the first rock albums to feature the instrument, released months before *Switched-On Bach*.

The problem was that operating the machine was not simple, evidenced by the fact that both John Lennon and Mick Jagger gave up on theirs. Many of the popular musicians that played Moogs, as well as the smaller, cheaper Minimoog that came afterwards, never learned how to use it outside of the confines of their genres. For example, Stevie Wonder, a huge proponent of the Moog, was still making funk and soul music with the instrument—excellent, golden, shimmering soul music, but soul music all the same. By contrast, the Berlin School musicians like Tangerine Dream and Klaus Schulze were creating a new genre using the instrument by reaching for the cosmos.

In his book, *Times & Sounds: Germany's Journey from Jazz and Pop to Krautrock and Beyond*, Jan Reetze makes the point that because groove and swing did not come naturally to German musicians, it was easier for these Berlin School musicians to ignore what was happening outside their country and create a new language from scratch. Reetze also makes the point that the synthesizer was not as widely adopted in America because of authenticity: "Synthesizers, as the unions saw them, were devices that could imitate conventional instrumentals and replace the musicians who played them. They perceived synthesizers as crutches for people who couldn't play a real instrument and thus were not fully valid musicians." This anti-synthesizer mindset was not limited to America. Queen, for example, notably placed a "No Synthesizers!" tag on their albums in response to an erroneous comment made by *Melody Maker*'s Chris Wels who mistook Brian May's guitar effects for a synthesizer, but the end result was the same: it was better to distance themselves away from an instrument that audiences may have perceived as "cheating."[2]

Origins

Born in East Prussia on June 6, 1944—D-Day as it so happened—Tangerine Dream founder Edgar Froese moved to West Berlin after the war. Froese originally took piano lessons, but eventually switched to guitar before studying painting at the Academy of Arts. Dissatisfied with visual arts however, he returned to music, forming his first band called the Ones, who released a lone single in 1967, "Lady Greengrass" / "Love of Mine," where Froese played guitar. According to Froese, the rest of the band had "no interest in following my experimental path into the different worlds of music," and so the Ones disbanded.[3]

That said, Tangerine Dream fans interested to hear where Froese came from should visit the A-side of the Ones' single, which evokes his future band's name by accident: "Puff the grass is tangerine / Puff the sky is suddenly green," his bandmate

Charlie Prince sings, evoking the psychedelic air of '67. The word "tangerine" appears in another song that same year: in the Beatles' "Lucy in the Sky with Diamonds," where John Lennon sings, "Picture yourself in a boat on a river / With tangerine trees and marmalade skies," which Froese misheard as "tangerine dream."

Froese's biggest influence in his formative years wasn't any musician, but Salvador Dalí, whom Froese met in 1965 through a friend and classmate who was then studying under the surrealist.[4] "Dalí was quite a big influence in my life because his philosophy of being as original and authentic as possible had touched me very intensively at that time," Froese remarked in an interview with *The Quietus* in 2010. "As he used to be incomparable I invested a lot of time, too, in training myself to follow such a philosophical path."[5] Tangerine Dream would be Froese's avenue to be "as original and authentic as possible." Whereas the Ones was derivative, Tangerine Dream sounded like nothing else.

At a small bar in Berlin called Zwiebelfisch, Edgar Froese and his then-girlfriend (and later wife), Monika, witnessed a band named Psy Free, which consisted only of an organ player and a drummer. The drummer's name was Klaus Schulze. Impressed that Schulze could hold a steady beat over a long time, Froese approached the drummer and extended an invitation, not only to join Tangerine Dream, but to join them for the upcoming Essen Song Days festival. Schulze agreed.

By Froese's account in his autobiography, *Force Majeure*, the set "punished the crowd with some archaic German underground culture that went over a lot of their heads. Our lecture—high up the scale of what one would normally be able to tolerate—was an explosion of atonal strangeness."[6] Underneath the onslaught of feedback, Froese recalled hearing

Schulze's dutiful beating of the kit, just as he witnessed that day at Zwiebelfisch. Tangerine Dream was later joined in October 1969 by former Kluster member Conrad Schnitzler.

The Early Years

Tangerine Dream's debut album, *Electronic Meditation*, was recorded privately in a factory in Berlin. The album name is misleading: the band had not yet procured a synthesizer, and so they created noise by other means, including Conrad Schnitzler on addiator, a mechanical German calculator. The tapes were not intended for public release but found their way to Paul Meisel, who released the album through Rolf-Ulrich Kaiser's Ohr label in 1970.

Kaiser may be the single most important figurehead in the discussion of kosmische musik, both for the music he released on his labels Ohr, Pilz, and Cosmic Couriers, and for organizing the Essen Song Days festival where Tangerine Dream performed live. Ohr also released the various artists compilation *Kosmische Musik* in 1972, containing songs by Popol Vuh, Klaus Schulze, Ash Ra Tempel, and Tangerine Dream, the biggest names in the genre.

Both Schnitzler and Schulze would soon leave Tangerine Dream, with the latter leaving and co-founding Ash Ra Tempel. Schulze was replaced by former Agitation Free drummer Christopher Franke, who would go on to be one of the most important members of Tangerine Dream when he began playing the Moog synthesizer, but that would not come for another few years.

In the interim, Tangerine Dream released three more albums on Ohr. *Alpha Centauri* was the first Tangerine Dream album to start their fascination with space—spelled out in song titles like "Sunrise in the Third System"—a concept that was more realized through the double album that came after, *Zeit*. *Zeit* is free-floating: each of its four songs occupies an entire length of vinyl on its own. For *Zeit*, Berlin-born multi-instrumentalist Peter Baumann is now part of the group, and in addition to Franke and Baumann on VCS3 analog synths, Popol Vuh's Florian Fricke is responsible for the Moog's first appearance on any Tangerine Dream album. *Atem* (1973) would be their last album on soon-defunct Ohr, and the heavy tom-toms from Christopher Franke on both the title track and closer "Wahn" represent the intersection of krautrock and the kosmische. It was also their breakthrough: Tangerine Dream fan and BBC radio DJ John Peel praised *Atem* as one of the best albums of the year, which got the attention of Virgin's Richard Branson who later signed the band.

The Virgin Era

Tangerine Dream flew to London to record their first album on Virgin, *Phaedra*, which is now regarded as a cornerstone in electronic music. Recorded in the same Manor Studio that yielded *Faust IV* and *Tubular Bells*, *Phaedra* is also the first album by Tangerine Dream that features their trademark synthesizer not played by an outside member.[7] The Moog that Christopher Franke plays on the album was originally owned by the Rolling Stones' Mick Jagger, who sold it to German producer Peter Meisel, who intended to use it for pop hits before Franke convinced him to sell it to Tangerine Dream using their advance from Virgin.[8]

To listen to *Phaedra* is to listen to what remains an extremely futuristic album, and so it's hard to imagine what audiences must have felt back in 1974, but that also explains its rare popularity for a purely instrumental album: *Phaedra* hit number fifteen on the UK charts, where it remained for fifteen weeks. Like so much krautrock, it was popular outside of Germany and niche in their home country, where it sold a modest six thousand units. Like their previous albums, *Phaedra* was completely improvised. "I can't remember there ever being a big discussion about the music itself. It just fell into place," keyboardist Peter Baumann recalled.[9] Christoph Franke was playing on the Moog sequencer when Baumann was in the control room and began recording him, unbeknownst to Franke, which is how *Phaedra*'s title track was born. The song's heady pulse has been co-opted by so much electronic music that followed it, be it television or film soundtracks to dance-floor invitations. *Phaedra* marked the start of Tangerine Dream's "Virgin era," where albums like *Rubycon* and *Stratosfear* further refined *Phaedra*'s sequencer- and synthesizer-based sound.

I'd go far as to compliment both latter albums as stronger pieces of work. Eventually, *Rubycon* rewards listeners with a similar pulse, but it's the atmospheric build-ups on both sides that distinguish it. The first side contains slippery tones that recall the album cover, like listening to water droplets dispersing in slow motion. Meanwhile, the second side brings in what sounds like samples of sirens that have been pitched lower and slowed down, drawing a connection between this pioneering electronic group and the shadow of World War II. They had never abandoned organic instruments, even as their albums became more electronic heavy, but *Stratosfear* seems to tip the scales a little to bring out the former more. There are more traces of guitar, harpsichords, piano, and even harmonica. This leads to some arresting moments where the band pairs up these natural sounds with artificial ones, such as the shorter interlude "Big Sleep in Search of Hades," which uses a mellotron flute to pastoral effect over a harpsichord chord progression.

Stratosfear was their last studio album with Peter Baumann. Altogether the band would go through many personnel changes, but one thing remained constant: Edgar Froese's leadership. The albums immediately following *Stratosfear* attempt to broaden Tangerine Dream's sound to varying levels of success. Released in 1978, *Cyclone* brings in drummer Klaus Krieger and England-born singer Steve Joliffe (of the British band Steamhammer), and the electronic magic of Froese and Franke often feels like it's supporting Joliffe instead of the other way around, which is likely why Joliffe doesn't appear on 1979's *Force Majeure*. The 1980's album *Tangram* starts approaching new age music, and the first song feels like its building toward something across its twenty-minute runtime, only to liberally take from the Who's climax of "Won't Get Fooled Again."

Like Can, Tangerine Dream's classic lineup of Froese, Franke, and Baumann was also short-lived. However, fans of the Virgin era received a huge gift in 2019 when Virgin released *Oedipus Tyrannus*. Originally recorded in 1974 to soundtrack the stage play, *Oedipus Tyrannus* is a deeply ambitious work spanning seventy-four minutes. The album also features both the space-ambient early sound of Tangerine Dream pre-*Phaedra* in "Act 1," as well as new sequencer sound in "Act 2: Battle," and so would have been the biggest Tangerine Dream album in scope.

Under Froese, Tangerine Dream released over a hundred studio albums and soundtracks, which doesn't even broach the subject of their many, many live albums or Edgar Froese's solo discography that he began exploring in 1973. On January 20, 2015, Froese passed away from a pulmonary embolism. Since his passing, the current lineup of Tangerine Dream— Thorsten Quaeschning, Ulrich Schnauss, and Hoshiko

Yamane—have kept the (no better word for it) dream alive under Quaeschning's leadership. While some fans were not happy about Tangerine Dream trucking on without Froese, in an interview with *Pennyblackmusic*, Quaeschning clarified, "It was not our or my decision to continue Tangerine Dream after Edgar's sad passing in 2015. He made plans for everything and also for this scenario together with his wife Bianca."[10] It makes sense: to Froese, Tangerine Dream was never about its people, but about being authentic and cosmic. Their albums since Froese's death have sparked renewed interest in the band, and yielded some of their strongest material in decades.

5 The Ancient Heavenly Connection: Ash Ra Tempel

Origins

When a 22-year-old Klaus Schulze left Tangerine Dream, he happened upon guitarist Manuel Göttsching and bassist Hartmut Enke at the Beat Studio in Berlin. Enke had just gone through the painstaking trouble to procure four WEM (Watkins Electric Music) speaker cabinets from Pink Floyd roadies in England, and brought them back to Berlin with him by train. As the WEM speakers allowed them to be the loudest band in all of Berlin, Schulze's curiosity was immediately piqued, and the trio formed Ash Ra Tempel on the spot, which would go on to be one of the most acclaimed Berlin School bands.[1] Unlike Tangerine Dream, who sought to distance themselves from rock music, Ash Ra Tempel were the golden mean between earthly krautrock and the cosmic Berlin School.

The name Ash Ra Tempel is made up of the English word "Ash," "Ra," referencing the Egyptian Sun God, and "Tempel," the German spelling of the word "Temple."[2] The words and their etymologies highlight the band's spiritual overtones, but also their stylistic range. Unlike Amon Düül II, who also invoked an Egyptian deity in their name, Ash Ra Tempel had no reservations about using English and German words in their name. Thus, in addition to representing the intersection of death ("Ash"), rebirth ("Ra"), and worship ("Tempel"), their name also signaled their interests in English, German, and Egyptian cultures. This is further represented in their debut album's foldout cover, which contains images of a pharaoh's head, as well as the opening lines of Allen Ginsberg's "Howl" printed in both English and German.

Born in Berlin in 1952, Manuel Göttsching was exposed to both classical music (because of his mother) and American soul music. Göttsching and Enke had spent time together first as a British Invasion cover band named the Bomb Proofs, before becoming the Steeplechase Blues Band. As the Steeplechase Blues Band, they were heavily influenced by blues, particularly the heavier blues of Eric Clapton and early Fleetwood Mac. And by using the blues as the basis to explore the cosmos, Göttsching's most obvious inspiration was Jimi Hendrix. Even when Göttsching and Enke formed Ash Ra Tempel, they never left the blues behind in the way that Edgar Froese left behind rock. Ash Ra Tempel's albums are generally sequenced to feature guitars on the first side and then spacey synthesizers on the second side, as if to say that their cosmic psychedelia was a natural extension of blues music.

Ash Ra Tempel's classic lineup of these three musicians was extremely short-lived, producing only their self-titled debut, released on Ohr in 1971. After that, Klaus Schulze departed, picking up his own synthesizer and starting a successful solo career as one of the greatest artists of Berlin School. *Ash Ra Tempel* is only comprised of two songs. The first, "Amboss," spans twenty minutes and is a series of climaxes upon climaxes. Considering how much power the band is able to get out of only three musicians, the track aligns them closely with fellow Ohr trio Guru Guru. By contrast, the second song,

"Traummaschine" (translating to "Dream Machine"), features Göttsching and Schulze producing long, explorative drone sections on guitar and synth. Even when drums eventually appear halfway through the twenty-five-minute piece, they sound distant, buried underneath Göttsching's soaring guitar. If Schulze's mechanized repetition in his drumming represented the machine in the song title, then Göttsching's guitar represented the dream. Had *Ash Ra Tempel* been released three decades later, listeners would have called this music "post-rock" given its long build-ups and drone sections, demonstrating the influence of these German bands on completely unrelated genres down the road.

On the following album, 1972's *Schwingungen*, Wolfgang Müller replaces Schulze on drums, and the trio is further bolstered by session musicians contributing saxophone, bongos, and even vocals. On "Darkness: Flowers Must Die," they sound far closer to Can than before thanks to the relentless drums from Müller and the fever-daydream lyrics of one-time vocalist John L. (real name Manfred Peter Brück, who also sang briefly in Agitation Free) that recall Malcolm Mooney while evoking the death of the hippy dream ("Flowers must die") and the death of the self ("I want to be a stone / Not living, not thinking"). While *Schwingungen* is formatted similarly to the first album, the first side is split into two tracks, opening with a six-minute ambient blues song no doubt inspired by Fleetwood Mac's hit "Albatross."

For their third album, Ash Ra Tempel wanted to work together with American beat poet Allen Ginsberg. But after failing to get a hold of Ginsberg, Rolf-Ulrich Kaiser instead paired them up with psychedelic drug pioneer Timothy Leary, who was exiled from America at the time. The results of the collaboration are documented on the 1973 album *Seven Up*.

Once again broken out into two distinct sides, the title refers not only to Leary's seven stages of consciousness, reflected by the album's seven parts, but also to an LSD-spiked bottle of 7 Up soda that was present at the studio.

The Cosmic Jokers

By 1973, Rolf-Ulrich Kaiser's labels Ohr and Pilz had already gone under. Undeterred, Kaiser swiftly moved to set up Cosmic Couriers to continue releasing the music he loved. In 1974, the label released five albums by a band named the Cosmic Jokers, all of which were recorded the year prior. Comprising members from fellow krautrock band Wallenstein—Harald Großkopf and Jürgen Dollase—and Ash Ra Tempel's Manuel Göttsching and Klaus Schulze, there are two versions of the story of the Cosmic Jokers. In the first version, these albums were both recorded and released without consent from their musicians by Kaiser, who had supplied the musicians with plenty of hallucinogens and encouraged them to make music together. Later on, Kaiser would edit the jams into albums and release them under a new band name that these musicians were not aware they were officially part of. This is the version that the courts decided on when Klaus Schulze took legal action against the Cosmic Couriers label, finally putting an end to Kaiser's career in music. There is a well-traveled story of Göttsching going into a record store that was playing a Cosmic Jokers album on the speakers, and when he asked who was playing, he was told to his surprise and anger, that it was him. However, Göttsching has denied this, stating in an interview that he was well-aware of the recording and releases of the Cosmic Jokers; that there were contracts drawn and monies paid.[3]

Whatever the case, it's clear that Kaiser still treated this music with reverence. If this music did come from drug-fueled sessions, then we can thank Kaiser for taking the trouble of editing them into semi-coherent psychedelic trips. But even if the musicianship can be stellar—for example, the wide-eyed synth climax of "Kinder des Alls" on *Galactic Supermarket*—the music is mostly directionless, floating off into space and hoping that you eventually land somewhere. Compare *Galactic Joke* with Ash Ra Tempel's debut and you can see the shortcomings. Both albums are only two tracks, and similar in setup where the first one is bluesy and psychedelic while the second one is more ambient, yet *Galactic Joke* is never as intense or as interesting.

Ash Ra Tempel's debut has another point going for it compared to their later albums, which is that it's white-hot and unrelenting because the band was a power trio back then and did not bother with a vocalist. For their subsequent albums, a revolving door of vocalists destabilized their lineup and ultimately softened the sound. It didn't help that the lyrics sung by these vocalists tended toward banal, barely veiled references to psychedelic trips. On *Schwingungen*, John L. sung about a "lysergic daydream," while on the aptly titled *Starring Rosi*, Göttsching's girlfriend Rosi Müller contributed gently spoken word lyrics such as "Let yourself fall into the infinite." When Göttsching started his solo career, he no longer relied on generic lyrics to make his point as he found the cosmos well within his guitar's grasp.

Solo

His albums *Inventions for Electric Guitar* (whose cover presents it as both the sixth Ash Ra Tempel album *and* a Manuel

Göttsching album, the ultimate transition from band to solo career) and *New Age of Earth* (released under the alias "Ashra") are both purely instrumental and notably serene—far more tranquil than the electronic second sides of the Ash Ra Tempel albums. Released in 1975, *Inventions for Electric Guitar* sounds like Tangerine Dream's long and moody sci-fi epic *Phaedra*, except Göttsching manipulated his guitar to sound like the synthesizer. By contrast, 1976's *New Age of Earth* is performed almost entirely on synths. The title of *New Age of Earth* is prophetic: by putting these graceful synth melodies in an ambient context, Göttsching predicted so many new age-ambient albums to come.

That said, Göttsching's biggest claim to fame is not either of those albums, nor any of the albums he made with Ash Ra Tempel. In December of 1981, after a European tour with Klaus Schulze, Göttsching went into the studio to record whatever he jammed on the spot, as was his method. One hour later, he came away with what would have seismic influence in the most unexpected of places: electronic dance music. Released three years later in 1984, *E2–E4* is a live-in-studio album with no overdubs that takes as long to listen to as it did for Göttsching to record. This is not a mark against the album in the slightest. Instead, it speaks to Göttsching's innovation and precision that he could have so casually invented a masterpiece.

To listen to *E2–E4* is to hear ambient techno being made ten years before it was supposedly invented. Despite being presented as different songs, the album is one continuous fifty-eight-minute piece, and it became a surprise hit at New York City's Paradise Garage, a hugely important venue in both LGBTQ+ and nightclub history. Funnily enough, Göttsching's intentions were not to make a dance record, but to transport the New York City minimalists into the world of synths, later explaining to *Loud and Quiet*, "I didn't record it in the sense of a dance piece. The drums were very in the background, and it's not really a 'bom bom bom' bass."[4]

Still under contract with Virgin at the time, Göttsching had trepidation with releasing the album through them. Even though Richard Branson claimed the record could make him a fortune, Göttsching felt Virgin was becoming more commercial and would not have appreciated such an experimental release, thus *E2–E4* was released on his old bandmate Klaus Schulze's Inteam label, founded that same year. With its title referring to a common opening in chess, the album cover is that of a chessboard, and can actually function as one should you need it. (Göttsching, a chess enthusiast, has indeed played on the cover himself, in case you were wondering.)

Unlike his albums as Ash Ra Tempel, Göttsching's electronic albums are not classified as krautrock—after *Inventions on Electric Guitar*, there is no trace of rock to be found anywhere— but he would not have gotten there had it not been for his work with Ash Ra Tempel, testing out the synthesizers that would later be the basis of his trailblazing solo career. Göttsching's career then is a study of krautrock's legacy in miniature. At first beholden to British blues rock, Göttsching eventually assimilated that influence—along with that of the American minimalists—and created an entirely new language. To go from psychedelic blues rock to dance music might seem like an unfathomable leap, but to Germans forging their own path in musical history, it was just a casual step in a different direction.

6 Haunted Island: Agitation Free

Origins

As a mostly underground phenomenon, many krautrock bands never attained any commercial or critical success before drifting off into obscurity. Many had disbanded well before krautrock became internationally known or a signifier of experimental cool, only putting out one or two studio albums while active. For example, there was Gila, who explored a folksier side of krautrock. There was Out of Focus, far more political than the other, more popular krautrock bands from Munich. There was Xhol Caravan, who went into the deep end of relentless improvisation after rejecting American R&B.

Ignored or forgotten in a lot of krautrock literature, the story of Agitation Free is short, violent, and brilliant. They also deserve props for being one of the earliest bands in the genre, having formed in 1967. Despite some setbacks early on—guitarist Ax Genrich left after a few months to join Guru Guru, while original drummer Christopher Franke moved on to be one of the most important members of Tangerine Dream—Agitation Free eventually put out one of the greatest one-two punches of the genre before calling it quits in 1974.

Agitation Free remains unique in that they were a non-*kosmische* krautrock band based out of Berlin. Despite being the largest and most populous city in Germany—and despite being its capital—there are a relatively low number of internationally successful krautrock bands from Berlin compared to the major cities in West Germany, especially those not involved in the Berlin School of electronic music. This was because of location: Berlin is located in East Germany, and was in the middle of the Soviet Zone. To be a band in Berlin at the time and tour West Germany, you had to drive two hundred kilometers through East Germany to get there, which added to the difficulty, founding guitarist Lutz Graf-Ulbrich explains to me on a Skype call.

Born on November 30, 1952, Lutz Graf-Ulbrich remembers growing up in Berlin quite well. "I remember that we were in school, and all of a sudden, they built this wall. That was a big shock for everyone," he says of the Berlin Wall. "It was so crazy and unbelievable that this could happen. And also, we were supported by the forces of France, England, and America: they had soldiers in town. We didn't understand why they didn't react to the Russians who built this wall, and everyone just watched. That was really strange."[1]

Graf-Ulbrich would become a guitar player only after he heard the Beatles' version of Chuck Berry's "Roll over Beethoven," prompting him to ask his father to buy him an electric guitar. "I wanted to be a rock and roll star," he muses.

> That's how I started. Later on, in the late '60s, we tried to create new music by ourselves. In the beginning, every German band sounded like English or American bands and we tried to copy them and learn their songs. But Tangerine Dream, Ash Ra Tempel, and the other krautrock bands—they were tired of copying American bands. We tried to play our own music.[2]

Predating many of the more acclaimed krautrock bands that formed the year after, Lutz Graf-Ulbrich formed Agitation Free in 1967 with Christopher Franke to do just that—play their own music—when they were just teenagers. Franke came from a musical family, and his mother taught violin. Graf-Ulbrich had met Franke in childhood: they were in the same kindergarten and would play music together at the age of twelve.

Agitation Free's influences and origins share remarkable similarities to that of Can, whom they later met and toured with. The way Lutz Graf-Ulbrich remembers it, fellow Agitation Free guitarist Lutz Ludwig Kramer had returned from England where he saw a Pink Floyd show. Concurrently, the band's music teacher and mentor, Swiss composer Thomas Kessler, introduced them to what the American minimalists like Terry Riley and Philip Glass were doing across the ocean.[3] Had Lutz Ludwig Kramer gone to America instead and saw the Velvet Underground, they would have a very similar story to that of Can. Instead, Agitation Free carved out their own lane in Berlin.

Kessler did more than just turn these young teenagers onto American experimental music. He also established the Beat Studio in the basement of a school in the district of Wilmersdorf, and allowed Agitation Free to rehearse there. Though the studio was simple, it became an important part of the Berlin School history when Tangerine Dream and Ash Ra Tempel recorded there.[4]

Agitation Free were also the house band of Zodiac Free Arts Lab, the infamous experimental venue where they met the members of Kluster. Graf-Ulbrich recalled that

> We were playing there in the evening. There was a theatre above, so you couldn't play loud music and so the concerts

started late. We were very young, 15 or 16 years old at the time, and we played until four in the morning! So I can't remember how we got through school the next day, but we played there quite often as Agitation Free.[5]

Though they formed in 1967, they had not yet landed a recording contract, and when they got a chance to release a record under Rolf-Ulrich Kaiser's Ohr label in 1970, their lineup was in flux, and so they missed the opportunity. Kramer was replaced by Ax Genrich, who was subsequently replaced by Jörg Schwenke. In spite of their childhood history, Christopher Franke was likewise replaced by drummer Burghard Rausch when Franke left for Tangerine Dream.

You Play for Us

These new members were joined by bassist Michael Günther, and synth, keyboard, and steel guitar player Michael Hoenig. Through Hoenig, they were also one of the few krautrock bands to get their hands on a synthesizer relatively early because it was so expensive. By contrast, bands like Xhol Caravan and Kraftwerk had to manipulate other instruments to get a similar synthetic sound. When I asked Lutz how Hoenig acquired the EMS Synthi A that he plays on their debut album, *Malesch*, he recalled that

Thomas Kessler was a very inspiring teacher for us. He was the first guy who told us, "You should have a synthesizer." At the time, we didn't really know what he meant because it was a new instrument that nobody had heard of. So we were one of the first bands in Germany that had the synthesizer which made this crazy sound that no other band had.[6]

Like fellow krautrock bands Can and Embryo, Agitation Free were deeply curious about other sounds and cultures, as evidenced by the name of their 1972 debut album, *Malesch* (Arabic for "take it easy"). Before making the album, the band was exposed to Indian music, as was trendy among British and American bands of the time, in addition to embarking on an international tour sponsored by the Goethe Institute: "We had just made this beautiful tour as the first rock band in the Near East, Egypt, Cyprus, Lebanon and Greece. That was a big impact on our music. Michael "Fame" Günther had recorded sounds on his transportable Uher tape recorder which we used to create the first world music sound."[7]

You can hear parts of their trip incorporated into the introductions of "You Play for Us Today," a comment made by the group's pilot when they were en route to Cyprus ("I fly the airplane, and you play for us"), and "Sahara City," which captures the bustle of the Egyptian streets. The band had a vision for blending these disparate sounds with American minimalism and psychedelic improvisations, and then framing them in this new context of an unheard German rock music. Many of the album's songs, while relatively short (especially in comparison to Can or Ash Ra Tempel), are constructed as one long crescendo. Songs like "Ala Tul" and "Pulse" demonstrate the influence of the minimalists via Michael Hoenig's synthesizer and sequencer, while condensed into five-minute songs. Thanks to the trip that the band took to those countries, *Malesch* stands out as one of the worldliest albums in the krautrock universe.

By contrast, their second album—simply titled *2nd*—aligns themselves far closer to what was happening in West Germany.

Also released on Vertigo, *2nd* is a far different album than *Malesch* thanks to the contributions of new guitarist Stephan Diez, who joined only to promptly leave the band after recording. Songs like "First Communication," the second part of "Laila" and "In the Silence of the Morning Sunrise" show both incredible polish and melody-precise guitar playing that the first album may have lacked. Meanwhile, the first halves of "A Quiet Walk" and "Haunted Island" align themselves with the proto-ambient experiments of so many other Krautrock bands around this time.

Despite finding a prompt replacement for Diez in Gustl Lütjens, Agitation Free disbanded the year after. Lutz tells me,

> Everyone has their own ideas of how we should play or which direction we should go. The bass player wanted to play in the Grateful Dead direction. The guitar player at the time liked jazz music, and wanted to make jazz-rock. Michael Hoenig, he was more into avant-garde music, like minimal music. Burghard Rausch wanted to play straight rock, and I was a hippy music fan. So we all had our own ideas. And so when Michael Hoenig had the opportunity to play with Tangerine Dream on tour and to play with Klaus Schulze, that was a big step for him.[8]

That was the end of Agitation Free for a long time. Graf-Ulbrich briefly joined Ash Ra Tempel, having known Manuel Göttsching since he was twelve because they had the same guitar teacher.

> When Agitation Free split up in 1974, I stayed in France. I came to listen to Manuel's album *Inventions for Electric*

Guitar, and I was so impressed by this record because it was a new step playing with echo. Of course, everyone used echo as a guitar player if you were into experimental music, but the way he did it was combining echo method with minimal music, and playing this minimal music on electric guitar was a new step for me. I called him and said "Hey, I'll come back to Berlin and let's have a session and let's play this music."[9]

After the Berlin Wall finally fell, Agitation Free reunited in the late '90s, yielding a third album, *River of Return*. When I asked Lutz about the circumstances that led to the reunion, he told me that it was because of his 45th birthday. Performing at the former train station in the middle of Berlin known as the Tränenpalast (Palace of Tears), Lutz celebrated his birthday with members of Ash Ra Tempel and Agitation Free.

We rehearsed one afternoon, and it was really great to play this music again, and we had so much fun that Gustav Lütjens, one of the guitar players, asked us, "Hey, the spirit is still there. Why don't we play and record a new album together?" The only problem was Michael Hoenig, who lived in Los Angeles for a couple of years already, and he was so busy that he couldn't join, so we didn't have him in the band. But we found a good producer and we started playing together and recording this album.[10]

Released in 1999, Agitation Free's third album *River of Return* looks fondly back at the band's classic sound while also testing the waters of what could have been. Songs like "Susie Sells Seashells at the Seashore" and "177 Spectacular Sunrises" are lengthy ambient explorations that the band had previously touched on in the first half of "A Quiet Walk," but are now full-fledged compositions. Meanwhile, to replace Hoenig, the band brought in a few guests to bolster their core quartet, including multi-instrumentalist Bernhard "Potsch" Potschka and Kraan saxophonist Johannes Pappert, and it's these friends that make songs like "River of Return" and "2 Part 2" far more interesting than they would have been otherwise.

Before he moved to California, Michael Hoenig's brief stint in Tangerine Dream was a major stepping stone. As such, Hoenig's debut album, *Departure from the Northern Wasteland*, sounds like Tangerine Dream's Virgin-era albums with its arpeggiated sequencer patterns. The twenty-minute title track, with Hoenig adding in layers slowly such that the song feels like it's building toward its quiet release of its conclusion, feels akin to the Philip Glass minimalism that inspired Agitation Free in the first place. Released in 1978, it's a relative latecomer to the Berlin School but should not be missed. After moving to Los Angeles, Hoenig turned to film, TV, and video game soundtracks, including composing the music for *The Blob* and some of the *Baldur's Gate* games, while Graf-Ulbrich kept busy as a banjo and guitar player in the folk band 17 Hippies.

"Haunted Island" is the name of the closing song on Agitation Free's second album, and while they did not know it at the time, it would end up being the final song from Agitation Free for many, many years until *River of Return*. As its name suggests, it is—until the drums kick in partway through—pure atmosphere, painting a sonic image of what it was like to live in Berlin at the time. "We were living like an island [in Berlin]," Lutz Graf-Ulbrich tells me, "and there were not so many bands here. But the whole situation, the end of the '60s, the politics and the music was developing new sounds and looking for new sounds, breaking rules with the revolution and hippy thing. We were looking for new things in every direction."[11] Agitation Free found those new sounds in American minimalism and a trip to the East, and brought them back to Germany to become one of Berlin's most fascinating if short-lived bands.

7 Electric Junk: Guru Guru

Origins

Born in Munich on the very last day of 1940, Mani Neumeier is the drummer, founder, and proverbial center of Guru Guru. As the years went on, other members rotated in and out, but Neumeier remained, the de facto heartbeat of the band. Unlike Agitation Free, Guru Guru's discography is vast: originally formed in the southwestern city of Heidelberg as the Guru Guru Groove in 1968, Guru Guru have put out over two dozen studio albums and are still active to this day.

There are many similarities between Can's Jaki Liebezeit and Neumeier. Notably, both drummers came from a jazz background. In Zurich, where Neumeier began gigging as an amateur musician, he was able to see many of the American jazz masters perform, including Louis Armstrong, Miles Davis, John Coltrane, and Art Blakey, experiences that he considers among the greatest moments of his life. He eventually began playing professionally as a member of the Irène Schweizer Trio, backing the Swiss free jazz pianist, and proudly considers himself the first free jazz drummer in Europe.[1] The other member of the Irène Schweizer Trio was bassist Uli Trepte, who would go on to form Guru Guru with Neumeier.

You can hear both Neumeier and Trepte playing with Irène Schweizer on the 1967 album *Jazz Meets India* alongside the

Dewan Motihar Trio—an early marriage of the seemingly disparate genres of free jazz and classical Indian music that predates Alice Coltrane's *Journey in Satchidananda* by a number of years. Furthermore, like Liebezeit, Neumeier had developed an interest in Indian music, specifically drumming that he learned from Indian percussionist Paramashivam Pillai. Finally, like Liebezeit, he eventually moved away from free jazz. In an interview with John O'Regan for *Ptolemaic Terrascope*, Neumeier made clear that the influences for Guru Guru were vast and eclectic, ranging from jazz musicians such as John Coltrane, Thelonious Monk, and Miles Davis, to the ethnic music of India and Africa, to the psychedelic bands of the late '60s.

In its early days, the band had tested out different configurations, including guitarists Edi Nageli and Jim Kennedy, saxophonist Rudi Sparri, and vocalist Hans Sax, but it was not until Ax Genrich joined that the band's first iteration was fully complete. Born in 1945, Axel Genrich, later known simply as Ax Genrich, would eventually be regarded as one of krautrock's fiercest guitar leads. But Genrich wasn't always a guitarist as he originally played electric bass before changing his mind after hearing the Rolling Stones. Before Guru Guru, Genrich played in many different bands. During his brief tenure as member of Agitation Free, he caught Guru Guru performing live in Berlin without a guitarist and asked if he could join in during the intermission. Guru Guru agreed, but they didn't have a guitar on hand. With no driver's license, Genrich asked his friend to quickly drive him home to get his guitar and then drive him back, whereupon he plugged in and started playing. That was Genrich's trial by fire into Guru Guru.

The Genrich Era

The world's introduction to the band came shortly after when Guru Guru's debut album *UFO* was released by Ohr in 1970. In the recording studio, Mani Neumeier invited some friends who played no instruments, just to add to the pungent marijuana smoke that emanates from the album's general atmosphere. Genrich's improvisations may occasionally recall Jimi Hendrix, but the sound is far heavier and closer to early metal in terms of volume and unrelenting intensity. The lack of compositional ethos can be seen in the band's unwillingness to give "Girl Call" a proper ending, instead building up only to snap directly into the lumbering "Next Time See You at the Dalai Lhama."

Hinten came the following year, also released on Ohr. Of their first two albums, *Hinten* takes the edge thanks to involvement from preeminent krautrock producer Conny Plank helping Genrich apply overdubs. No song title better exemplifies the band's approach than "Electric Junk": it might have sounded like junk to some people, but no one could argue that it wasn't electric. (They were also working toward being the funniest band from the German underground, as seen in the album cover of *Hinten*, where the band name is tattoed on a man's buttocks, or when they named a song after Bo Diddley that sounds absolutely nothing like the early American rock and roller.)

I was able to connect with Genrich over email, and when asked about his experience working with Conny Plank, he replied, "Working with Conny was love at first sight. As an engineer, Conny was more engaged than [*UFO* engineer] Tom Müller. He gave lots of room and time for my playbacks and helped me with my self-confidence. It was a real production, more sophisticated than *UFO*. I'm still proud to be on it."[2]

Hinten was their last album on Ohr. Citing disagreements with label head Rolf-Ulrich Kaiser, the band made the move to the newly formed Brain label for their third album, *Känguru*. The album cover—a mother kangaroo asking "Käng Käng" to its pouched infant who replies "Guru Guru!"—is unmistakably reminiscent of a similar "dialogue" that appears on the cover of Pavement's 1995 album *Wowee Zowee*, once again demonstrating Stephen Malkmus's love of krautrock. The album is similarly composed of sprawling ten-minute songs, but Ax Genrich's guitar has been peeled back, making room for humorous vocals from Mani Neumeier, hence the song title "Immer Lustig" ("Always Funny"). *Känguru* would be the last album with bassist Uli Trepte, who, according to Neumeier, "wanted to take over and write all the compositions without Ax and me."[3] Genrich didn't stay much longer either, leaving after the group's self-titled fourth album in 1973 and launching his own solo career thereafter.

Rotate

Given how important Genrich's guitar was in the first iteration of Guru Guru, one might have expected the band to falter when they replaced Genrich. However, any misgivings were quickly addressed on 1974's *Dance of the Flames*. There, Neumeier recruited electric guitarist Houschäng Nejadépour, who came from a jazz fusion outlet called Eiliff, and even played briefly with Kraftwerk. Nejadépour does not merely slip into Guru Guru's sound, he takes and runs with it, channeling Jimi Hendrix as much as Genrich did, while bass duties are handled by Trepte's replacement, the Switzerland-born Hans Hartmann. Alas, that would be the only Guru Guru album Nejadépour would perform on.

After his time with Guru Guru, Genrich had moved to Berlin but eventually made his way to Conny Plank's studio out near Cologne.[4] The results of these sessions were released under the name Highdelberg, which featured friends Genrich invited to partake, including his old bandmate Mani Neumeier and members of the groups Kraan and Cluster. An alternate cover of their one and only album announces "AX GENRICH HIGHDELBERG SUPERSESSION" in bold and colorful letters to make it clear that it's Genrich's album and not Neumeier's, who released *Mani und Seine Freunde* ("Mani and His Friends") around the same time with many of the same musicians. People expecting more of the lengthy guitar workouts of Guru Guru may be shocked at Highdelberg's tunefulness. For example, "Odenwaldpolka" is a feel-good instrumental dance with a country romp bass, and even "Kosmische Phyrze," the album's longest song, is characterized by Genrich's melody-focused electric guitar. To its detriment, the album never scorches, nor truly makes use of its collaborators.

Meanwhile, Mani Neumeier has never stopped drumming, either in Guru Guru or his many side projects, including Gurumaniax (where he once again collaborated with Ax Genrich) and the Damo Suzuki Network in the late '90s. Guru Guru's latest album, *Rotate!*, was recorded in 2017 as Neumeier was approaching eighty years old. And as of writing, he shows no signs of slowing down. Ultimately, it is bands such as Guru Guru that best demonstrate krautrock's tenacity.

Fritz Scheyhing, mellotron player of the krautrock band Gila, once described the impact of Guru Guru:

With Guru Guru we saw the first German free-rock band perform and heard for the first time how a band could shake the walls with turned up amplifiers—a completely new way of making music: not playing nicely together at a moderate volume level but making a hall full of people freak out. That was exactly in line with our mood. Music, ecstasy, power, and getting carried away.[5]

A good comparison to early Guru Guru would be the early records of Ash Ra Tempel, another guitar-bass-drum trio with little or no concerns for vocals. Both trios were able to create an overwhelming mass of sound with few instruments, but whereas Ash Ra Tempel sought transcendence via drugs, Guru Guru had no such aspirations. It was just music, reinforced by drugs, or perhaps the other way around.

8 Universal Believer: Popol Vuh

Origins

Born on February 23, 1944, in the lake-dwelling island town of Lindau, Florian Fricke would be among the first-ever people in Germany to own a Moog synthesizer. The second person to be exact, after composer Eberhard Schoener, who was also Fricke's neighbor and responsible for introducing Fricke to the instrument in the first place. The Moog was famously expensive at this time, but Fricke's upper-class background allowed him to procure one. Because of his early adoption of the instrument, Fricke's band Popol Vuh would have undoubtedly been connected to the Berlin School musicians had they formed in Berlin instead of Munich. However, Popol Vuh's most important records—and where their musical legacy resides—came after Fricke sold his Moog to Tangerine Dream's Klaus Schulze and switched from electronic instruments to acoustic ones.

Taught to play the piano as a child, Florian Fricke was a prodigy, going to a specialized school for music when he was much younger than his classmates and winning piano competitions. But like many other krautrock musicians, his life was changed when he discovered free jazz after moving to Munich. In 1969, he formed Popol Vuh with his wife Bettina Fricke, percussionist Holger Trülzsch, and sound designer Frank Fiedler. The band name comes from the sacred Mayan book of creation, which signified "a spiritual revolution" for Fricke that occurred alongside the counterculture political movement: "The culture of the old Maya, of the book 'Popol Vuh,' was one way for us to find ourselves, re-define our ideas in early days," he said in a rare English interview with Gerhard Augustin.[1]

Studio Albums

Working for Liberty/United Artists Records, producer Gerhard Augustin heard about the Moog and wanted to produce an album with it. This resulted in Popol Vuh's first album, *Affenstunde*, an exploration of the different sounds that Fricke could wrestle out of the machine. For the most part, the tones are gentle, bordering on ambient with the exception of "Ich Mache Einen Spiegel Dream Part 5," where Trülzsch's percussion is at its most prominent. Their second album, *In den Gärten Pharaos*, can be seen as the transition from electronic instruments to acoustic ones, thanks to the use of the organ on the second song, "Vuh," recorded live in a church.

By their third album, *Hosianna Mantra*, Fricke had completely abandoned the Moog. Where the Moog once allowed him to explore new and unheard sounds, it was ultimately too much of a hindrance for Fricke, who never truly mastered the instrument in the ways his Berlin School contemporaries did, later stating that he didn't think it was appropriate using electronic instruments to play the deeply spiritual music that Popol Vuh would soon embrace. Thus, after playing the instrument as a guest on Tangerine Dream's *Zeit* and on Gila's *Bury My Heart at Wounded Knee*, he sold his Moog to Klaus Schulze in 1975, enabling the ex-Tangerine Dream and Ash Ra Tempel drummer to launch his own solo career.

It's on *Hosianna Mantra* where Popol Vuh really come into their own as one of Germany's most rewarding bands: whereas their first two albums bear resemblance to the early Berlin School records, *Hosianna Mantra* is so totally unlike anything the other radical German musicians were making. Similar to Ash Ra Tempel and contemporaneous Munich band Amon Düül, the name *Hosianna Mantra* is a combination of different languages and, in this case, religions: Hosianna, from Christianity, and Mantra, from Hinduism. While the album name implies heavy religious music, Fricke made clear in that same interview that while "a conscious reflection upon religious origin is included in this music," it was "not in particular to any religious groups."[2]

The magic of the album mostly comes instead from the new additions to the band, including Gila guitarist Conny Veit, oboist Robert Eliscu, tambura player Klaus Wiese, and soprano singer Djong Yun, daughter of notable South Korean composer Isang Yun. These instruments alone demonstrate how far removed they were from their contemporaries; *Hosianna Mantra* is purely chamber music, not at all synthesized and certainly not rock music in the slightest. "Kyrie" is a masterpiece of pure texture, where guitar notes from the young Veit weep over Klaus Wiese's drone, recalling the works of Alice Coltrane around this time, while Yun's vocals reach high up toward the heavens.

After *Hosianna Mantra*, the Berlin-born Daniel "Danny" Fichelscher, also of Gila, would join the band as another guitarist and drummer. Born in 1953, Fichelscher was quite young at the time of Popol Vuh's next albums *Seligpreisung* and *Einsjager & Siebenjager*, leaning hard on the crash cymbals and aligning the band far closer with rock music than they had ever been. Adding to this on *Seligpreisung* is Florian Fricke's endearingly amateurish vocals—taken up in the absence of Djong Yun, who was in America at the time of recording— which are more in line with what you would hear in far more "traditional krautrock" sound, oxymoronic as that phrase may be. Fricke regretted his vocals later on, which explains why he again returns to an instrumental role on the following *Einsjager & Siebenjager*. Danny Fichelscher was also a member of fellow Munich band Amon Düül II, whose singer Renate Knaup would join Popol Vuh later on.

Even when Fricke was singing lead, the vocals were never the focal point. Like other krautrock bands before them, Popol Vuh were purely a textural band, which Fricke described as "a group of people who make music but are not a music group," at once recalling the democratic structure of groups like Can and the communalism of groups such as Amon Düül and Embryo.[3]

Soundtracks

Popol Vuh's songs were epic in scope and yet reserved in volume, which made them perfect for film soundtracks, and so equally important to Popol Vuh's legacy is their musical contributions on twelve films by Werner Herzog. Born in Munich on September 5, 1942, Herzog would soon become one of Germany's most famous directors. Popol Vuh's first film soundtrack was for Herzog's international breakthrough, *Aguirre, der Zorn Gottes* (*Aguirre, the Wrath of God*), which came to be after Fricke and Herzog met in 1967, back when Fricke was working as a film critic. "We worked closely together," Herzog recalled about Florian Fricke in the book *Herzog on Herzog*, and often I would tell him the story I had in mind before there was even a written screenplay. We wouldn't talk about music; we spoke instead about the inner drama of the story, or about some sort of vision I had. He was a poet first and a musician second, and his feel for the inner narrative of a cinematic story was infallible.[4]

The first sound we hear on *Aguirre* is the high, heavenly notes of Florian Fricke's choir organ for the movie's establishing shots above the clouds. From there, the camera slowly descends until we see the sixteenth-century Spanish expedition making their way down the mountain and into the jungle in search of El Dorado, the fabled city of gold. Herzog explains his musical vision for the film:

> I wanted choral music that would sound out of this world. Florian used a strange instrument called a choir-organ, which is similar to a mellotron and contains three dozen different tapes running parallel in loops. Each tape would be a voice of a single pitch. Put together it sounds like a human choir, but the music has an artificial, eerie quality to it.[5]

By using the prerecorded sounds of this instrument, Fricke contributes heavenly tones that brings with it a foreboding atmosphere because the artifice is noticeable—an effect that would not have been achieved had Fricke relied purely on the human voice. Thus, though there is a clear contrast between the spirituality of Popol Vuh's soundtrack and lack of spirituality in Aguirre and his conquistadors' journey in the film, proving Fricke clearly understood Herzog's "inner narrative."

Fricke would continue to work with Herzog regularly, soundtracking the films *Herz aus Glas* (*Heart of Glass*), *Nosferatu*, and *Fitzcarraldo*, among others, although the two slowly drifted apart after 1987's *Cobra Verde*. "[T]owards the end we moved in different directions," Herzog recalled, "he drifted into New Age pseudo-culture and the style of his music changed. I used to joke with Florian, telling him, 'You must never grow old. You have to die young and beautiful.' I can still hear those words in my mind today."[6] Near the end of 2001, Florian Fricke passed away from a stroke. Despite stating that Popol Vuh were not a music group, Fricke was always Popol Vuh's leader, to that point that Popol Vuh was always Fricke. Unlike Tangerine Dream that could soldier on without Edgar Froese, when Florian Fricke died, that was also the end of his band.

While the Berlin School musicians were forging a national identity by embracing the synthesizer, Popol Vuh did the opposite: they forged their own unique identity by rejecting the machine. And whereas the early Ash Ra Tempel records looked for cosmic transcendence through drug consumption, Popol Vuh represented a different side of kosmische musik, seeking transcendence through spirituality. "There's no doubt about it that my music has delighted a lot of people who were into drugs or smoking or taking trips or whatever, that was part of our musical culture in those days. And my music was especially geared towards this clientele," Fricke said in the same interview with Augustin. "But I did not make the music because of that."[7]

Perhaps the best example of Popol Vuh's spirituality and calm is told by Fricke's widow and Popol Vuh member Bettina von Waldthausen, who said in an interview with Jason Gross for *Perfect Sound Forever*, "I believe Florian's deepest wish was to touch the heart. And that is what happens if you listen to Popol Vuh, even after so many years: it can bring you in your heart. Someone wrote to Florian. 'My baby cried all night. I didn't know what to do. But when I played *Hosianna Mantra* it stopped at once.'"[8]

9 Made in Germany: Amon Düül II

Origins

A large number of krautrock bands emerged from communes, which makes sense: krautrock wasn't just music, it was cultural. Such bands included Cluster/Harmonia, Embryo, Faust, Guru Guru, and, most prominently of all, Amon Düül II. Communes can be broadly defined as groups where all members live together and share similar beliefs and values, and is certainly not limited to German bands. For example, prominent communal bands from North America include Jefferson Airplane and the Grateful Dead.

As their name suggests, Amon Düül II originated from the West German political-musical commune Amon Düül (apt to cause some confusion, which is not helped when members of Amon Düül II refer to themselves simply as "Amon Düül") that originally had ties to Kommune 1, also known as K1, regarded as the first political commune in Germany.

Kommune 1 was founded on January 12, 1967, with nine adult members and one child whose objective was to simply share in each other's ideas and lives. When communal living proved to be boring, Kommune 1 took to acts of political satire, including a failed "pudding assassination" of then-US Vice President Hubert Humphrey in which they planned to pelt the politician with pudding, yogurt, and flour. The subsequent press made them a national sensation, and even got coverage overseas in America.

Later on, K1 would be known for their hippy lifestyle, particularly when Munich model and future German sex symbol Uschi Obermaier joined. Under Kommune 1, the private was made public: there were no lavatory doors, and telephone conversations were run through a loudspeaker so that everyone could hear.[1] Meanwhile, Obermaier spoke openly about her sexual relationship with fellow Kommune 1 member Rainer Langhans, turning them into a notable countercultural power couple, sometimes regarded as Germany's own John Lennon and Yoko Ono.

Kommune 1 was short-lived, lasting only two years and being put to bed for many reasons, including founding member Dieter Kunzelmann's heroin addiction leading to his expulsion, as well as the raiding and destruction of their communal living area from a gang of bikers. As a result, some of the members of K1 formed Amon Düül, a musical commune that focused on playing music together, even if that did not mean playing well.

The name "Amon Düül" was deliberately chosen to avoid any German or even English connection: "Amon" refers to the Egyptian deity, king of the Egyptian gods, while the word "Düül" is possibly the Turkish word meaning "duel." The original Amon Düül put out a few albums together, but guitarist John Weinzierl later admitted that they played music mainly out of necessity when the commune members' parents stopped sending over money: "there had to be a new source of income. As some members played an instrument, the decision to form up a band seemed logical."[2]

Amon Düül's debut album, *Psychedelic Underground*, could have been the name for this whole movement in Germany. For fans of Amon Düül II curious to see where they came from, no blues-based psychedelic workouts appear here. Instead, "Ein Wunderhübsches Mädchen Träumt von Sandosa" is seventeen minutes of relentless tribal drumming and call-and-response vocals. Piano parts wander in only to wander out of the critical mass, and the song feels like the genuine result of a commune that took up music: there is a primitive energy there that isn't present in the Amon Düül II records. Meanwhile, "Kaskados Minnelied" quiets down, combining an electric guitar riff and what sounds like a cello drone, while closer "Bitterlings Verwandlung" uses a crunchy guitar that the punks would have admired to let the album ride out in style. Despite the promising beginning, things were not meant to last for the first Amon Düül, which released a few more albums before some of its members, fed up with the politics, broke off to form Amon Düül II, a decidedly more "proper" band.

Amon Düül II's original lineup was different from most other bands. For one thing, because they originally came from a commune, there were simply more people in the group, and so Amon Düül II's debut album features two drummers, two bassists (although they don't play on the same track), two guitarists, and a female singer in Renate Knaup.

One of Amon Düül II's two guitarists was John Weinzierl. Born in 1949 to a musical family (his father was a zither player while his mother was an accordion player), Weinzierl grew up listening to classical music. He eventually formed a group called the Merseygents, covering British Invasion bands before developing an interest in the psychedelic rock of the late '60s, particularly Frank Zappa, the Doors, and Pink Floyd. Such bands would be the reference for Amon Düül II's albums to come. Weinzierl worked in tandem with other guitarist Chris Karrer, and the two alternated lead roles: "Usually, I played the lead on

Chris's tunes and he played the lead when I wrote the song," Weinzierl said.[3]

The Early Years

Amon Düül II's debut album is titled *Phallus Dei*, Latin for *God's Phallus*, which adequately reflects the band's attitude around this time: they did not want to be taken seriously, hence the absurd falsetto on "Dem Guten, Schoenen, Wahren," scatting on "Luzifers Ghilom" and problematic lyrics throughout on BDSM and pedophilia.[4] Sonically, they lean hard into the aesthetic of so many psych bands around this time, especially Pink Floyd. That said, like Can or Agitation Free, Amon Düül II did not want to limit themselves to a German, British, or American sound, opting instead to pull influences from sources like Indian music.[5] This is immediately apparent on *Phallus Dei*, where opener "Kanaan" features a guitar that has been disguised to sound like a sitar. (On their later albums, they'd bring in an actual sitar player in Al Gromer.) Meanwhile, "Kanaan" has Embryo leader Christian Burchard playing vibes over John Weinzierl's lumbering two-note bass, while the near twenty-one-minute title track becomes a lengthy tribal percussion workout halfway through. According to Weinzierl, the album was mostly improvised and then subsequently arranged, and it shows, as the playing is looser here than their future albums.

The core lineup remains the same for their second album, *Yeti*, except vibraphone-player Christian Burchard and second drummer Dieter Serfas are no longer there, having left to form Embryo. But the playing is different, more innervated, and the interplay between the band members tighter. Instead of

Phallus Dei's improvisational approach, there was a conscious decision to make an album full of normal, composed songs on *Yeti*.[6] What results is what is often considered the band's magnum opus. The song titles emphasize the strangeness of the psychedelic world therein: "Eye-Shaking King" and "Pale Gallery" read like titles of short horror stories, while "Soap Shop Rock" is comprised of parts with trippy names like "Halluzination Guillotine" and "Gulp a Sonata." Unlike Can or Neu!, Amon Düül II were interested in long-form pieces that were not lengthy, studio-edited jams but rather heavily composed works made up of shorter pieces or actual songs, hence "Soap Shop Rock" on this album, a four-part medley that forms the album's the first side.

Make no mistake however, *Yeti* is not a cerebral album. Much of its appeal is to hear the primal rhythms and searing guitar riffs. When record producer and talent scout Siegfried E. Loch ("Siggi" Loch) recounted the time he first saw Amon Düül II perform in 1969, he would liken them to "an early heavy metal band," and listening to the album's lead single and highlight "Archangels Thunderbird," it's obvious what Loch was referring to: the song seems to explode out of your speakers.[7]

But there are occasionally other textures. Chris Karrer's violin, combined with Peter Leopold's mortar shell-drumming, creates the eerie war atmosphere for the excellently titled "Flesh-Coloured Anti-Aircraft Alarm" portion of "Soap Shop Rock." Meanwhile, one-time Tangerine Dream flautist Thomas Keyserling features on closer "Sandoz in the Rain," as well as Ulrich Leopold and Rainer Bauer, members of the original Amon Düül. As Weinzierl remarked on their inclusion on the album's final song, "After we had become famous, we thought it would be a good idea to have a session together with former members on one of our Amon Düül II albums, just to let them play along for the sake of old times. This became 'Sandoz in the Rain.'"[8]

The cover of *Yeti*, depicting the band's sound-person Wolfgang Krischke as the grim reaper, would become one of krautrock's most renowned images when UK author Julian Cope used it as the cover for his book on the genre, *Krautrocksampler*. But had Cope gone with something else, *Yeti*'s cover would be striking all the same: after the photo was taken, Krischke passed away due to hypothermia sustained during a LSD trip, and the picture was selected as a tribute to him.

Most bands would have followed a double album like *Yeti* by pulling back a little bit and returning to the single album format, but Amon Düül II instead got more ambitious with yet another double album, *Tanz der Lemminge*, released the following year. Bongo-player Christian "Shrat" Thiele and bassist Dave Anderson are no longer here, having left to start other projects (Thiele formed lesser-known krautrock act Sameti, while Anderson returned to England and joined Hawkwind), replaced by Lothar Meld on bass and Karl-Heinz Hausmann on electronics.

Tanz der Lemminge would mark the first time that each composition is credited to individual members instead of the full band, having learned their lesson when they were shafted their dues previously. John Weinzierl considered himself and Chris Karrer to be the principal writers for the bulk of the Amon Düül II albums, but given their communal background, they shared everything, including songwriting credits. Looking back, Weinzierl considered attributing their early material to the full band as a mistake.[9] The first two sides are made up of one long, multipartite composition each. Karrer's suite, "Syntelman's March of the Roaring Seventies" is far more acoustic but still plenty psychedelic, reminiscent of David Bowie's *The Man Who Sold the World* in parts. Meanwhile, Weinzierl's suite, "Restless Skylight-Transistor-Child" is far looser; the results are less congruous but ultimately more fascinating.

Amon Düül II had a very productive year in 1972, but then again, so did just about everyone else: in addition to Amon Düül II, Al Green, Alice Coltrane, Banco del Mutuo Soccorso, Embryo, Gentle Giant, Lou Reed, Matching Mole, Ornette Coleman, Premiata Forneria Marconi, and Stevie Wonder all put out two albums apiece. Aretha Franklin and Deep Purple put out two as well, if you count their live albums, as did Lô Borges if you count the album he made with Milton Nascimento. Something special was clearly in the air that year. But not only did Amon Düül II release *Carnival in Babylon* and *Wolf City*, they also toured England—twice—the first of which was their first successful tour of the country, and the second of which was captured on the live recording *Live in London*, released the following year.[10]

Whereas Amon Düül II's early albums are a balance between composition and improvisation, *Carnival in Babylon* is the demarcation point. Going forward, improvisations are restricted within the confines of tighter songs; gone are the side-long epics of their previous albums. But the band seems cautious on *Carnival in Babylon*, and the album doesn't rock nearly as much as anyone might expect from them. By contrast, *Wolf City* is confident, louder, and faster. "Surrounded by the Stars" could be their best song, psychedelic by way of sensory overload. Lothar Meid's bass gallops while D. Secundus Fichelscher's drums tumble and slash, both creating a bracing rhythm for the band's two guitarists. American-born organist Jimmy Jackson—associated more with fellow Munich krautrock band Embryo—plays the choir organ, creating the illusion of the sunrise that Renate Knaup sings about on the song. "Green Bubble Raincoated Man" recalls the strangeness of Jefferson Airplane's "White Rabbit" in lyrics like "Just an advice: don't ask your face tonight," before the band cuts loose in the song's face-melting second part. "Wie der Wind am Ende Einer Strasse" is a beautiful instrumental deserving of its romantic title ("The Wind at the End of a Road") while also demonstrating the band's complicated relationship with Germany: it is one of the two songs on the album with a German title, yet sounds nothing like German music thanks to the inclusions of Al Gromer on sitar and Shankar Lai on tablas, demonstrating the band's resolve to be multicultural.

The Mid-Era

Often ignored completely in critical explorations of the band's discography, 1974's *Hi-Jack*—released as *Hijack* by Atlantic, dropping the album's half-baked pun—is a tepid affair lacking the psychedelic immersion and artful folksiness of their previous records. This is in part because it's also the first Amon Düül II album not produced by Olaf Kübler, who was able to get so much juice and acid out of their sound on the previous albums. (Kübler still appears, playing flute and saxophone on the album.)

But the band gets ambitious once more on the following *Made in Germany*. In many ways, *Made in Germany* can be heard as the group's last hurrah and attempt to crossover Europe and into America. Potentially inspired by the surprise success of Kraftwerk's *Autobahn* in the United States, Amon Düül II, who had previously distanced themselves from their German roots for so long, opted to make a consciously German album, replete with references to well-known German figures and even a satirical interview with Adolf Hitler using clips of Hitler's speeches in "5:5:55."

Alas, any great songs like "Emigrant Song," with its multipart harmonies, are buried underneath the weight of the album's over-conceptualization and what Chris Karrer would later lament as "strong nationalist overtones," satirical or not.[11] The twenty-one-song album was intended as a double concept album in the style of the Who's *Tommy*, including a five-minute instrumental overture likely inspired by German composer Richard Wagner, but it was only in Germany where the album was released as intended. In America, Atlantic Records released a ten-song version, voiding the concept. The German version also features the full band donning costumes of historical figures on the cover, while the American release features a lone Renate Knaup, striking a sexy pose à la German actress Marlene Dietrich, likely in a vain attempt to lure listeners in.

It didn't work. Not only did *Made in Germany* fail to chart, but it also marks the spiritual end for the band. In an interview with Andy Whittaker in the now-defunct *Delerium's Psychedelic Website*, John Weinzierl recalled,

> After *Made in Germany* the Amon Düül system was breaking down; we weren't living together, there were crises all the time. Everyone had hassles. Amon Düül had been a family, but disillusion had set in, lot's [sic] of different lineups. Then we had a situation of producers wanting Amon Düül to produce music; they didn't understand the idea of the band, that it was the mouth of something. But as usual, business bought it all—all the youth movement was bought up, and it died as a result.[12]

Made in Germany: Amon Düül II

The Late Period

The albums that came after don't sound like they were made by the same band, which was partly because that was indeed physically the case. On 1976's *Pyragony X*, Karrer, Weinzierl, and Leopold are joined by Klaus Ebert on bass, who used to be a part of the rock band the Petards, and Stefan Zauner on keyboards, who would go on to form the new wave act Münchener Freiheit. Like the late-period Can albums, when Can was joined by members of Traffic, the sound of *Pyragony X* has an unnatural fluorescence, and both *Pyragony X* and *Almost Alive*, released the year after, sound faceless by what was once one of the most unique psych bands in the country. In that context, 1978's *Only Human*'s feels like the band trying to absolve themselves of any blame: they were, after all, "only human," and everybody makes mistakes. Guitarist John Weinzierl had called it quits after *Almost Alive*, and (again, like Can) Amon Düül II turned to disco, which may seem like a death knell move for a psych band, but they sound more confident in this new territory than they had on their previous albums. "Kismet" is a late-career highlight, an eight-minute centerpiece featuring a Middle Eastern influence in Chris Karrer's guitar wash.

Released in 1981, *Vortex* can be heard as Chris Karrer's Hail Mary attempt to revitalize Amon Düül II into the new decade, going so far as to bring Lothar Meld and John Weinzierl back into the fold. But the '80s production stifles a band like this, as Daniel Fichelscher's plodding drums suck the life out of everything around it. When *Vortex* failed to generate much interest, Amon Düül II disbanded, although a reissue of an album called *Utopia* was released under the name Amon Düül II the year after. If you happen to find a copy of *Utopia* with the words "Amon Düül II" on the cover, don't be fooled: it is not an Amon Düül II album (even if some of them guest on a few tracks) but rather one by producer Olaf Kübler, whom Weinzierl later accused as "trying to make more money with our name."[13] The original release of *Utopia* in 1973 was under Kübler's short-lived alias Utopia, after United Artists' mostly Jewish bosses did not care for the band name Kübler originally proposed: Olaf & His Electric Nazis.[14] Neither Utopia nor Amon Düül II's last few albums do enough to tarnish their reputation as the German underground's most formidable psychedelic band.

Though Chris Karrer had explicitly stated his intention for the band was to be multicultural, the band was ultimately nowhere near as eclectic as Can or fellow Munich band Embryo.[15] Any Indian influence on their debut album was quickly superceded by heavy psychedelia reminiscent of British and American bands like Pink Floyd and Jefferson Airplane as early as *Yeti*, which would be the prevailing sound going forward. So when Weinzierl says that Amon Düül II weren't a krautrock group, I understand where he's coming from. Except krautrock is supposed to be German bands finding their way through a cultural void, and in that regard, Amon Düül II are krautrock through and through.

10 World Fusion: Embryo

Origins

More than any other band discussed in this book, Embryo embraced sounds, cultures, and musicians from across the globe, and brought them into their unique version of krautrock. The number of musicians who have played together with Embryo total over four hundred, and so Embryo should be considered less of a band and more of a collective of musicians, and in that regard, they embodied a different way of communalism than Amon Düül.

Embryo was formed in Munich in 1969 by drummer Christian Burchard and saxophonist and flautist Edgar Hoffman. However, the roots of the band sprouted as early as 1956 when a young Burchard befriended Dieter Serfas at school in Hof. The two jammed together, playing jazz and rhythm and blues. Because there was the presence of the American military in Hof, Burchard was introduced to different American jazz styles there, and was eventually given a vibraphone, which would become his primary instrument.[1]

Burchard and Serfas would both play on Amon Düül II's debut, *Phallus Dei*, but even before that, they had performed on an album with pianist Mal Waldron, Prestige's in-house pianist in the late 1950s who played for Billie Holiday and Charles Mingus. Having played Waldron's compositions before

Burchard even met him, Burchard considers Waldron to be a "big influence."[2] Together with three different bassists on different tracks, including Amon Düül II's Lothar Meid, Waldron, Burchard, and Serfas recorded *For Eva* in 1967, which would be released as an Embryo album almost three decades later in 1999. Thus, even before Embryo's proper debut, they were already steeped in American music that the Nazis would have frowned upon. Even back in the Hof days, Burchard and Dieter enjoyed playing with Black American soldiers: in an interview with *It's Psychedelic Baby! Magazine*, Burchard recalled "some of them were musicians and especially the black among them were jamming with us."[3]

The Early Years

Embryo's official debut was named *Oval*, released via Ohr in 1970 and recorded in only two days.[4] The influence on Christian Burchard from his Amon Düül II days looms large and it's ultimately thanks to Edgar Hoffman that the album manages to carve out its own distinct category of German rock-jazz fusion. Hoffman's saxophone dominates the album—it's the lead "voice," especially since the actual vocals tend to be downplayed whenever they are there. And when Hoffman isn't playing sax, he plays electric violin, contributing to the eerie atmosphere of "You Don't Know What's Happening," an effect compounded by the heavy tom-toms from Burchard. At times, the song feels like a cross between 1960s psych rock and 1980s post-punk, and in many ways, krautrock was the bridge between those two disparate genres.

Multi-instrumentalist Roman Bunka joined the band around the time they recorded their second album, *Embryo's Rache*, and though he's officially credited with playing bass, he has clarified that he doesn't play a single note on that album.[5] Instead, the bass parts are handled by American jazz player Jimmy Jackson, who also plays organ on the record. Whereas *Oval* sounded similar to the psychedelic rock of Amon Düül II, *Rache* marks a radical departure for Embryo as there is no guitar. Instead, filling out the sound are mellotron and organ played by session musicians Jimmy Jackson and Mal Waldron. This is in stark contrast to their third album, *Father, Son and Holy Ghosts*, where Embryo did not make use of any additional musicians. Furthermore, on *Father, Son and Holy Ghosts*, with Christian Burchard not bothering with keyboard, they are reduced to a keyboard-less quartet, but the band members diversify their instruments such that there's no shortage of color: bassist Dave King doubles up on flute and marimba while guitarist Sigi Schwab also plays the Indian veena and tarang.

Between 1971 and 1972, Embryo recorded a lot of material that was ultimately rejected by United Artists and released later by Brain. These songs materialized in the albums *Steig Aus* and *Rocksession*, where they had fully embraced being a jazz fusion band, while also incorporating more "ethnic" elements which would heavily appear in their albums moving forward. *Steig Aus* opener "Radio Marrakesch/Orient-Express," for example, is heavily influenced by their travels to North Africa.

Embryo also recorded *We Keep On* in the last month of 1972 with American saxophonist Charlie Mariano (who played on the Charles Mingus albums *The Black Saint and the Sinner Lady* and *Mingus Mingus Mingus Mingus Mingus*). Released on the BASF label the following year, *We Keep On* is notably less jam-heavy than the Brain albums, but is otherwise just as musically curious. "Abdul Malek" opens the album with African percussion, while Mariano picks up the nagaswaram, a South Indian wind instrument. The album cover, featuring a cracked egg floating in the sky, would become yet another significant image of krautrock thanks to its use as the cover to Nikos Kotsopoulos's book, *Krautrock: Cosmic Rock and Its Legacy*. Albums such as these would later prompt Miles Davis to comment on them, "That German hippy group where Mal Waldron used to play; they are doing interesting things. You know, man? They are good musicians, just playing good shit!"[6]

Those years in the early 1970s yielded some of Embryo's best albums, but they have continued to put out albums in the fifty-odd years since. They waved goodbye to rock music on 1977's *Apo-Calypso* and fully embraced being world travelers on 1979's *Embryo's Reise*, a double album containing song titles such as "Straße nach Asien" (which translates to "Road to Asia"), "Far East," and "Hymalaya Radio" alluding to an eight-month trip to India that Embryo had undertaken around this time, captured in the documentary *Vagabunden-Karawane*. And then in the 1980s, a trip to Africa yielded collaborations with the Yoruba Dun Dun Ensemble on the 1985's *Embryo & Yoruba Dun Dun Orchestra* and 1987's *Africa*.

Marja's Embryo

In 2018, Christian Burchard passed away, leaving the reins of Embryo to his daughter, Marja Burchard, who grew up with the band and first appeared on stage with them when she was eleven. The last album that Christian Burchard played on was 2016's *It Do*, by which point his daughter already began composing songs for the band. The album's title references the hippy slogan "do it" but flipping it into the new phrase, *It Do*, which appealed to Christian Burchard's love of Dadaism.

It Do is thirteen songs long, which allows it to showcase different artists, including Indian-born vocalist Bajka harmonizing closely with the short song's strange synthesizer on "Maroc Mix," originally a Mal Waldron composition. When I got the chance to speak to Marja Burchard about her relationship with Waldron, she said,

> Mal Waldron was very close to us. My father always called him a musical father, so he was my musical grandfather. When I was around seven or eight, Mal Waldron was still living in Munich and had children my age. He came to our place and he played piano, and I played piano with him together, so we did four hand improvisations together. He taught me a lot of stuff, but more spiritual and emotional than technical. I mean, I heard his playing, and it influenced me a lot, but he never told me "you have to do this or that." It was more like his presence and his playing taught and inspired me.[7]

Embryo's first album under Marja's leadership was *Auf Auf*, its title a love letter to Christian, who loved the German expression which literally translates to "Up up," or, "Keep going." *Auf Auf* was released on the label Madlib Invazion, which hip-hop listeners might recognize as the one founded by producer Madlib in 2010. While the connection may be surprising, Madlib is a huge Embryo fan, considering them his favorite rock band.[8] Marja estimates that she and her father met Madlib around ten to fifteen years ago. "Madlib somehow got in touch with my father to ask if they could work together. My father was always a little bit skeptical, like 'who would want to come to me?' But he was very happy to see how interested Madlib was, and how much knowledge Madlib had of different kinds of music," she told me. "He found out Madlib really knew everything, and my father was very happy to meet him. For my father, it was a big lifestyle to hear a lot of music and to educate himself through music, and that's what Madlib was doing also. He was kind of a preacher of good music for young people, which is very important."[9] They jammed together, and were supposed to play together in concert in Berlin but unfortunately Madlib got sick and could not come.

Auf Auf is faithful to classic Embryo, bringing in musicians from other parts of the world, including Abdul Samad Habibi playing the rubab, a lute-type instrument from Afghanistan, on "Baran" as well as Embryo veteran Roman Bunka playing oud, a Persian string instrument, on "Besh." Immaculately produced and mixed, the album sounds at times like it could have been released on the Munich jazz label ECM. Unfortunately, it would be the last album that Roman Bunka played on; he passed away on June 12, 2022, from cancer. "I traveled with Roman in the beginning of this year. We went to Pakistan, India, Sri Lanka, and Bangladesh, to places he traveled with my father in the '70s. It was very beautiful and emotional," Marja told me, calling Roman part of her family.

> I've known him since I was born. He was a very inspiring person, and an amazing musician. Roman met my father when he was eighteen, and my father must have been around twenty-five. Roman always looked up to my father, because he was giving him new ideas, and new music. My father came from a jazz background, and Roman came from rock.[10]

Given Embryo's history of absorbing music from other cultures, I asked Marja if Embryo were ever criticized for cultural appropriation, and she confirmed that such criticisms have been constant. "If you look properly inside our structure and our respect between each other, it's not the right place to use that term, but people are often on the surface and don't look deeper," she says to me, giving an example of Embryo working with a musician from Afghanistan for the past twenty years.

He's living here in Munich but has no job. The state has not treated him well, and he's not respected as much as he had been before the war in Afghanistan. We are playing with him, and meet with him very often to learn from him and to show him our respect towards his culture and his music, and to give him a big space here and feature him and his amazing music. We also recorded one song with him, and sometimes he calls me his German daughter. When people tell me this song is culturally appropriated, I'm very sad because it's the contrary: it's a big appreciation of him, and the personal connection we have. It's completely out of context to use that term, and it's very dangerous to use these words if you don't know the proper relations of people towards each other. And it's a little bit sad because if you see the history of Embryo, you see that they never used music to make money. They always exchanged their ideas.[11]

Christian Burchard's legacy is a band that knew no geographical borders, genre restrictions, or language barriers. If krautrock could not so easily be defined, then Embryo is krautrock through and through: a German band that played global music.

11 A Beat That Lasts Für Immer: NEU!

Origins

If krautrock's most notable feature is supposed to be its motorik beat, then Neu! deserves credit for inventing it. There are better drummers than Neu!'s Klaus Dinger, but it's Dinger's lack of technical expertise that allowed him to invent a beat that was so simple yet effective, which he dubbed the "Apache beat." Can's motorik drummer Jaki Liebezeit played as if he had two sets of arms, so that Can's songs feel like they could groove forever. By contrast, Neu's songs feel like they could *chug* forever. Ultimately, it's perhaps no surprise that motorik's simplicity came from a drummer that learned how to play by bashing about with spare wood while learning carpentry, and not a superhuman on the kit like Liebezeit.

Neu!'s name—stylized as NEU! and pronounced "noy"— translates to "New!" in German. The name was chosen, according to Dinger, because "at that time [Neu!] was the strongest word in advertising."[1] Their album covers all appear as simple marketing posters, the word "NEU!" against a simple background. Neu! are composed of only two principal members, Klaus Dinger and guitarist Michael Rother.

Dinger is the older of the two, born in 1946 in Scherfede, Westphalia, Dinger moved to Düsseldorf when he was one. Before he became a drummer, he studied architecture in art school and learned carpentry under the tutelage of his father. In fact, his first experiences with percussion were as a carpenter—banging on pieces of wood—until he eventually bought a drum kit and started playing American rock as part of the groups the No and the Smash, before moving on to free jazz.

Michael Rother, on the other hand, was born in Hamburg in 1950, and lived in Pakistan in the 1960s before eventually moving to Düsseldorf. As a guitarist, he was heavily influenced by Jimi Hendrix and Eric Clapton.[2] Prior to Neu!, Rother played guitar in a band called Spirits of Sound alongside Wolfgang Riechmann and Wolfgang Flür. (Flür is best known as a member of Kraftwerk.) In contrast to the music he would soon make in Neu!, the music of Spirits of Sound was inspired by the British Invasion bands. However, like the other krautrock bands, Rother sought to create his own sound: "The development of my own personality demanded to create something individual. Imitating or interpreting other musician's ideas wasn't satisfactory any longer and that is why the English pop and rock music clichés had to be abandoned and overcome," Rother said in an interview with *Perfect Sound Forever*.[3]

In 1970, Kraftwerk were partway done recording the debut album of Kraftwerk when their original drummer Andreas Hohmann left them, so they asked Dinger to play on the final song. It's through Kraftwerk that Dinger met Michael Rother, who joined Kraftwerk shortly after him, and together they left to start their own band. This was partly to do with Dinger not being a fan of the direction Kraftwerk was heading, and partly to do with a perceived difference in their classes. He considered himself a "working-class hero," while he viewed the more privileged members of Kraftwerk as "millionaires."[4]

Neu!'s early days were uncertain. At the time, Michael Rother was also studying psychology as an alternative career path, and it was not until Dinger met with Conny Plank where they decided to go to the studio and record their first album.[5] There being only two members was less a conscious decision than a necessity. "[W]e didn't see any other chance at that time, there were not so many people like that; for instance today, the younger generation here is much easier to find people to understand musically or work with together," Dinger said of the limited collaborators at their disposal, explaining, "everything else was far away from what we wanted to do. But I think we somehow found, especially during this work with Florian, we somehow found what we wanted to do alone."[6]

With only two members contributing vocals, bass, guitar, drums, and other instrumentation, Neu! automatically became a studio band that relied heavily on overdubbing and electronics—far more than Can, who also used studio editing but could still jam out on stage. Neu! tried to perform onstage with prerecorded material using a cassette recorder, but the practice was frowned upon by audiences at the time. They moved to performing with other musicians, including bass players like Guru Guru's Uli Trepte and Kraftwerk's Eberhard Kranemann, but eventually gave up playing live altogether.[7]

In krautrock producer Conny Plank, however, Neu! had a not-so-secret third member. If you look at the credits of any German record from the 1970s, it's a good bet that it has Plank's fingerprints on it, whose résumé includes production or engineering work for Cluster, Kraftwerk, Ash Ra Tempel, Guru Guru, and Scorpions, not to mention artists outside of Germany like Brian Eno, Devo, Ultravox, and Eurythmics. Not only did Plank have the technical know-how and studio access Rother and Dinger needed, but he was also extremely enthusiastic for the new music they were making.[8]

The Original Trilogy

Their first album, *Neu!*, arrived in 1972, which was recorded across only four nights, as it was cheaper to rent a studio at night.[9] While the postrecording mixing and editing process was important for those early Can records, it was absolutely vital here. Without Conny Plank's guiding hand, it's safe to say that no one would have cared about these drums and guitars. But with Plank's touch, these organic instruments are organized in such a way that they sound synthetic while still retaining a natural glow: there is never any doubt that there's a human behind the heartbeat. The melodic tones on groovy opener "Hallogallo" sound so warm that you can practically swim in them. While other artists would use synth pads or keyboards to generate them, that's just the thing—there is not a single keyboard played on *Neu!* And so *Neu!* is ultimately proof of what you can create with so little: just guitar, bass, drums, and spirit of sound.

Album opener "Hallogallo" can be considered ground zero for the motorik beat. Spanning ten minutes, the track really hammers home this new idea of a drumbeat as the guitars weave texture and melody around it. Because the drumbeat was so deliberate, it made every drumroll feel that much more seismic by comparison. In a different context, those drumrolls may seem simple and not as special, but here, they feel like they can move earth. Appearing in the second half, "Negativland" is the longest song and can be considered "Hallogallo's" noisier, ill-tempered younger brother. The rest of the album is made up of proto-ambient songs that, in contrast to the electronic acts coming out of Berlin like Tangerine Dream, are far more earthbound due to being created with organic instruments instead of synthetic ones.

Neu! 2 came the year after, and it would have no doubt been a better album than their debut if they had finished it the way they envisioned. Neu! had rented out an expensive recording studio and used the time and money for the first half of the album, only to realize that the advance from the label would not cover them for the rest. Because *Neu!* wasn't exactly a huge moneymaker (Klaus Dinger estimates that it sold thirty thousand copies during the first two years), their record label Brain neglected to send more money. Desperate, the band just padded out what they had with remixes.

Like "Hallogallo," opener "Für Immer" is the draw, and it might be even better. The guitar isn't content to stand still. Instead, it tosses a tiny little melodic fragment into the air and lets it linger there, while the beat during the bridge has plenty of dub effects applied such that it feels like the song is shifting as it returns to the original chug. It also has the better name: "Hallogallo" is a meaningless play on the German greeting *Hallo* and the slang word *Halligalli*, which means "wild partying," whereas "Für Immer" translates to "Forever," which the song takes to heart as it pounds onwards for eleven minutes, a minute longer than "Hallogallo." Meanwhile, "Spitzenqualitat" contains cavernous-sounding post-punk drums that threaten to swallow the listener. The second side contains different remixes of the *Super* single that was released ahead of the album, including "Super 78," a ninety-five-second burst of high-speed music that would have been labeled punk rock had it been released a few years later.

Though Klaus Dinger and Michael Rother sound in sync on these records, their personalities could not have been further apart. On stage, Dinger bashed into his drum kit to the point that blood came out, captivating audiences. On the other hand, Rother was far more reserved. "I never felt the need for this kind of performance and always tried to come across with just the music. So I sat behind my few effect devices and pedals and focused on the developing music and not so much on the audience," he said years later. "In good moments the opposite worlds of Klaus and me came together at our recordings, with the help of Conny Plank, which should not be forgotten. I guess the tension of bringing together incompatible elements is what is fascinating people with NEU!"[10]

In June 1973, Michael Rother left Düsseldorf for Forst and co-founded Harmonia, only to return later to fulfill his contractual obligation with Brain to release three albums as Neu!, and because he had ideas that could not be realized with his new band.[11] The result was *Neu! '75*, which concluded their original trilogy. The approach for this new album was different than their previous albums. Not only did Rother bring in keyboards from his time with Harmonia, but the second side would be recorded in a four-piece band, including two drummers, Dinger's brother Thomas Dinger and Hans Lempe, to take over Klaus Dinger's role. This was Klaus's idea, who wanted to be at the front of the stage playing guitar and singing as the prototypical front man.[12]

The two sides of *Neu! '75* are as different as the band's two leaders. The first side is far more ambient, a refinement of the quieter songs on their debut but now informed by Rother's work with Harmonia. "Isi," with Rother's keyboard additions, feels like the happy medium between the two bands. Meanwhile, the second half rocks far harder and louder than anything the band had done prior. Imagine the shock for Neu! fans who would flip the record after the appropriately titled "Leb' Wohl" (an archaic German farewell), only to be met with the sudden onslaught of "Hero." While the two halves of the album may seem like they came from Rother and Dinger working separately, that is not the actual truth. Rother clarified in an interview with *The Wire* that "'Hero' and 'After Eight' … would have sounded different if I hadn't been working with him, just as 'Isi' and 'Seeland' wouldn't have been the same if Klaus hadn't joined his ideas to mine. I think it's a bad idea to try to separate that, because [we] always react to what the other does."[13]

Neu! '75 was the end of Neu! for a long time. Rother started his solo career while Klaus Dinger recruited the other two musicians of *Neu! '75* and formed La Düsseldorf. Fans of Neu! should continue Dinger's journey into La Düsseldorf, so named to avoid copyrights with the city name and for "a bit more glitter," according to Klaus Dinger.[14]

La Düsseldorf

La Düsseldorf's self-titled debut, released in 1976, sounds very much like where Neu! might go, albeit with less primal drums. The opening song, "Düsseldorf," for example, runs on simple melodies weaving around an elastic beat for twelve minutes, reminiscent of "Hallogallo" and "Für Immer." Meanwhile, "Silver Cloud," hit number two on the German charts despite being an instrumental, making La Düsseldorf more popular than Neu! ever was.

La Düsseldorf's second album, *Viva* (1978), and final album, *Individuellos* (1980), don't have the benefit of Conny Plank's production work, which may explain their glossier sound. The Dinger brothers are singing more, even though neither can carry a tune, and the chords themselves sound far happier than they ever did on Neu! With the volume and tempo both stalling out, there's no punk edge anymore, whereas the Neu!

records sounded like two musicians accidentally arriving at punk and post-punk years ahead of schedule. David Bowie once famously proclaimed La Düsseldorf to be the soundtrack of the 1980s, but ultimately their reign was short-lived: they disbanded in 1983, but their debut stands tall, merging Neu!'s motorik, optimistic beat with a cleaner sound.

Like La Düsseldorf, Michael Rother's solo career was more commercially successful than his work in Neu! For example, his first three solo albums all sold 150,000 copies each in West Germany. Rother's albums sound very much like a continuation of his work with Cluster's Hans-Joachim Roedelius and Dieter Moebius in Harmonia, featuring similar ringing guitar melodies backed by generous delay effects. His early records feature assistance from Can's Jaki Liebezeit, who channels an Apache beat that is eerily similar to the one that Klaus Dinger invented, albeit far more restrained as Liebezeit knows he's not the main attraction.

Dinger and Rother tried to put their artistic differences aside, reuniting Neu! in the mid-'80s. The reunion, lasting half a year, must surely rank among the shortest and least-fulfilling ever. The results wouldn't see the light of day for some time because they couldn't get record companies to bite, and so the album was shelved until 1995, when *Neu! 4* was secretly released by Klaus Dinger via the Japanese Captain Trip label without involvement from Michael Rother, who neither approved of its release nor felt it was good enough.[15]

When Dinger passed away, Rother would "fix" the album to his liking under the name *Neu! '86*, which was released in 2010. Of the two, *Neu! '86* is the ever-so-slightly more rewarding album by virtue of Rother removing the too-long, too-uninteresting collage experiment "86 Commercial Trash," but neither should be considered part of the Neu! canon.

Like Faust, Neu! are strictly a German band: they had very little interest in incorporating music from other countries, although Klaus Dinger did show an early interest in some ethnic music. On the first two Neu! records, he can be heard tinkering with Japanese instruments, including playing the koto on the intro of "Neuschnee," as well as what is credited as a "Japan banjo" on their first record but is actually a Japanese string instrument called a taishōgoto. In the late 2000s, after the dissolution of Dinger's latest band—la! NÊU?—he recorded an album with Japanese musicians and his new wife, Miki Yui, intending to release the album under La Düsseldorf but was denied permission by drummer Hans Lempe. Thus, Japandorf was born.

Japandorf

While Neu! aren't thought of as one of krautrock's many communal bands, Miki Yui noted that Japandorf was "not just making music together but being together," a sentiment echoed by the communal krautrock bands such as Amon Düül and Faust.[16] After Klaus Dinger passed away on March 21, 2008, from a heart attack at the age of sixty-one, Miki Yui added the finishing touches on the album, which would be released via Grönland under the band name "Klaus Dinger + Japandorf" in 2013. The album cover invokes nostalgia for the early Neu! records, which it resembles much more than the La Düsseldorf albums, featuring a simple pink rendition of the Japanese kanji symbol for "love" on a bare background.

The songs on Japandorf are cobbled together, with some songs dating back several years, while others are taken from jam sessions. There's also filler, including a throwaway Dinger spoken word track lasting twelve seconds, and two additions from Miki Yui, including the closer "Andreaskirche," which is just thirty seconds of ringing church bells as a tribute to her husband. The best songs are the ones that had been developed over the 2000s: "Immermannstraße," "Udon," and "Spacemelo." "Immermannstraße" is the only song credited to the full band, while the other two songs are credited to four out of the five band members. "Immermannstraße" and "Spacemelo" are both surprisingly twee and tuneful; the latter even has a guitar line reminiscent of the summer-humid guitar lines of Yo La Tengo. "Udon," named after the Japanese noodle, features drummer Masaki Nakao reciting the instructions of how to cook the dish, while the unceremoniously titled "Sketch No. 1_b" and "Sketch No. 4" are reminiscent of the monolithic motorik songs that Dinger once made with Michael Rother by his side, but now with Japanese bandmates.

Neu!'s music could only have been made by Germans; by Düsseldorfians specifically, as the duo assimilated the city's art scene and advertising culture into something new. Yet, Neu!'s influence has penetrated music outside of Germany, from David Bowie to Sonic Youth and beyond. Regarding his signature Apache beat, Dinger described it as "essentially about life, how you have to keep moving, get on and stay in motion."[17] There is something beautiful in that. In Dinger's hands, something as simple as a drumbeat becomes more than just a sound. It becomes a symbol, a reminder to keep moving.

12 We Are the Robots: Kraftwerk

Origins

Kraftwerk are a paradox: they are the most internationally renowned krautrock group, but they are also not known at all for their krautrock albums. Instead, they are known for what they made when they transitioned to using synthesizers, which helped popularize the instrument in mainstream music and created a model for so much electronic music to come. In the same manner that the classic rock artists of the 1960s inspired tons of hopefuls to pick up guitars, Kraftwerk inspired people to pick up synthesizers and drum machines instead, heralding not only the synth-pop wave that came soon after, but also any genre that did not bother with traditional rock instruments, including hip-hop, techno, and house.

Notably, *Artificial Intelligence*, the 1992 Warp compilation of embryonic IDM, or "intelligent dance music," depicted a robot slouching on a recliner listening to music, with the vinyl sleeves of Pink Floyd's *Dark Side of the Moon* and Kraftwerk's *Autobahn* strewn across the floor. Hip-hop pioneer Afrika Bambaataa and the Soul Sonic Force's 1982 song "Planet Rock" liberally sampled Kraftwerk songs "Numbers" and "Trans-Europe Express," while Run-D.M.C.'s Darryl "DMC" McDaniels said "Kraftwerk were a foundation of hip-hop not just because of their music, but they built their own machines and computers."[1]

But Kraftwerk are a paradox in another way too: they were the German band that became big outside of Germany while retaining their German identity in a way that their contemporaries did not. In an interview with Lester Bangs for *Creem*, Kraftwerk co-founder Ralf Hütter made this much clear when he pointed out that,

> We are the first German group to record in our own language, use our electronic background, and create a central European identity for ourselves. So you see another group like Tangerine Dream, although they are German they have an English name, so they create onstage an Anglo-American identity, which we completely deny. We want the whole world to know our background.[2]

Ralf Hütter was born on August 20, 1946, in Krefeld, northwest of Düsseldorf. His bandmate Florian Schneider was born on April 7 the following year, making them both part of the postwar generation. Schneider was the son of famous German architect Paul Schneider and writer Evamaria van Diemen-Meyerhof, a half-Jewish woman that Paul Schneider married against his Nazi father's will.[3] For people familiar with Kraftwerk's meticulously composed electronic pop albums, they may be surprised to learn that their origins date back to 1968 when Hütter and Schneider met in a jazz improvisation class at the Düsseldorf Conservatory.

Before Kraftwerk, Hütter and Schneider first formed a group named Organisation, which released one album, *Tone Float*, with the help of Conny Plank in 1970. *Tone Float* sounds nothing like Kraftwerk—in fact, it sounds detached from anything else happening in Germany. For one thing, though the kaleidoscopic cover art suggests yet another psych rock album, there are no guitars. Instead, Schneider's flute and Hütter's organ are joined by glockenspiel, bells, cowbells, and maracas played by the other musicians of Organisation: Basil Hammoudi, Butch Hauf, and Alfred "Fred" Mönicks. Thanks to Plank, the album was released by RCA in the UK (and only available in Germany as an import), but due to poor sales RCA dropped Organisation, which dissolved away, leaving Hütter and Schneider to their devices. One remnant of their former band remained, however: on the back of the cover of *Tone Float* was the image of a traffic cone, which would become the earliest symbol associated with Kraftwerk.

Archaeology

In November of that same year, Kraftwerk's self-titled debut album, which prominently featured the traffic cone on the front cover this time, was released on Philips. Schneider and Hütter were backed by two drummers in Andreas Hohmann and a pre-Neu! Klaus Dinger. That there were two drummers backing them was not a conscious decision à la Amon Düül II, but because Schneider and Hütter had trouble finding drummers that fit with their vision: they needed a drummer that would not overplay while also willing to embrace new technologies.

Of the album's four tracks, "Ruckzuck" impresses the most, whose song title—like Neu!'s name—creates a sense of urgency, translating to "Right Now." Knowing where Kraftwerk would go in just a few years' time, it is hard not to consider the title to be a boast, as if to say, "You are listening to the future, right now." "Ruckzuck" contains an absurdly catchy flute part from Florian Schneider, which locks into Hohmann's circular rhythm. Hütter is responsible for the breakdown, tossing concussive chords of organ near the middle before the rhythm starts up again.

Meanwhile, producer Conny Plank is behind the boards, and it's with his help that he's able to turn this strange band of flute, organ, and drums into a bona fide rock groove on "Stratovarius." Andreas Hohmann left Kraftwerk after the completion of "Ruckzuck" and "Stratovarius," so "Megaherz" is completely drum-less. Instead, the nearly ten-minute song is dominated by Hütter's organ, which sounds akin to the intense noise-making of early Cluster during the intro and outro, while the middle section is serene and beautiful as the warm tones envelop the listener in a gentle embrace. Klaus Dinger joins the band for closer "Vom Himmel Hoch," waiting until halfway through the song to start a drum beat that's far heavier than what Hohmann played or what Dinger himself would soon do for Neu!

When Hütter momentarily left the band in 1971, Michael Rother briefly joined the band, only to jump ship with Dinger and form Neu! before Kraftwerk's second album. Though the repeating pop art traffic cone cover art suggest a continuity between *Kraftwerk* and *Kraftwerk 2*, they do not feel akin in the slightest. Freed from any restrictions that a physical drummer would have placed on them, Hütter and Schneider are left to their own devices, testing out a drum machine for the first time on "Klingkang," as well as textural experiments such as "Atem," translated as "breath," a literal recording of slow breathing. The best of the album's tracks after "Klingkang" is the gentle, guitar-based "Wellenlange," whose guitar chords in the second half sound like they would inspire "Return" by Brian Eno and Underworld's Karl Hyde many decades later.

Their third album, *Ralf und Florian* (issued as *Ralf and Florian* in the UK with translated song titles), marks the end of

Kraftwerk's early period. Flutes, guitar, and organ are still prominent, but the duo get more mileage out of the rhythm machine while also testing the waters with synthesizers and what would later become the band's trademark robot vocals using an early vocoder. The cover illustrates the transition well: the traffic cone featured on their first two album covers is still here, but no longer the focal point, delegated to the band logo. Instead, the central focus becomes the two musicians, Florian Schneider—looking dapper with his perfectly combed hair, a tie, and even a music note lapel button—sitting side-by-side with Ralf Hütter, who didn't get the memo about dressing up. (He would get another opportunity on the cover of *Trans-Europe Express* where all members of the band would don suits to resemble mannequins.)

Ralf und Florian also moves away from the experiments of *Kraftwerk 2*, presenting six melodic offerings. "Elektrisches Roulette" has an elastic drum pattern and sounds like if sentient toys crafted a Neu! song. "Tongebirge" applies liberal reverb to Schneider's flute so that it feels like it's swirling, an effect compounded by the harmonies from Hütter's organ. "Heimatklänge" is a miniature ambient composition, and "Tanzmusik" hints at the far more danceable grooves the band would soon make (the name literally translates to "Dance Musik"). Whereas *Kraftwerk 2* started with its longest song, *Ralf und Florian* ends with its own, a far more enticing album sequence by saving its best for last: "Ananas Symphonie" is far and away their most idyllic composition at this point, painting a picture of a peaceful life full of pineapples and stainless steel appliances.

Kraftwerk would later disown their first three albums. Notably, they have not performed any songs from the first two albums since their 1975 *Autobahn* tour live, and have similarly stopped performing songs from *Ralf and Florian* after 1976. Schneider has disparagingly referred to this trilogy of sorts as "archaeology." But music fans are inherently part-time archaeologists by nature, unearthing forgotten or undiscovered gems, and digging up these albums allows listeners to see where Kraftwerk came from. The drums near the end of "Ruckzuck" sound like a train, predicting the concept of *Trans-Europe Express*, for example. Meanwhile, Kraftwerk named their famed Kling Klang recording studio and Kling Klang label, from where they recorded and released all their subsequent albums, after "Klingkang," their first song to make use of a drum machine.

More than that, these albums are simply worthy in their own right. Because the price of a synthesizer at the time was deeply prohibitive, musicians who wanted to achieve that electronic sound would resort to using cheaper instruments and liberally apply effects to them to make them sound artificial, which is exactly what Kraftwerk did. Synthesizers appear nowhere on *Kraftwerk* and *Kraftwerk 2*, and it was not until *Ralf and Florian* that Kraftwerk started using them. Instead, organs and electric flutes were stacked on top of one another and manipulated and distorted to sound less like their natural selves.[4] Early Kraftwerk was already hinting at blurring the distinction between the organic and the synthetic, and all three albums are great krautrock albums, even if they may not be great Kraftwerk albums.

Autobahn

If Schneider had his way, *Autobahn* would be considered the first Kraftwerk album. It was the album that brought them international attention when a single edit of the twenty-three-minute title track pared down to only three and a half minutes was played by a Chicago radio station. The single became Kraftwerk's biggest hit in the United States, reaching number twenty-five on the Billboard Hot 100 and leading to a tour across the Atlantic while also giving them more exposure back home in Germany. Interested in a single that broke through in America, "Autobahn" (in an even shorter single edit) also went to number nine in Germany. The parent album reached number five on the Billboard charts and number seven in Germany. It was also the first album with new member Wolfgang Flür, a drummer who had previously played in the Beathovens, a Beatles cover group that was popular enough to support the Who and John's Children in Düsseldorf, and then the Spirits of Sound with Michael Rother.

Autobahn is best remembered for its sprawling title track, which feels like a culmination of everything Kraftwerk had done up until this point. (By contrast, some of the shorter songs like "Kometenmelodie 1," "Mitternacht," and "Morgenspaziergang" feel like they could have appeared on *Kraftwerk 2* or *Ralf und Florian*.) The vocoders of *Ralf und Florian* that were used to add wordless harmonies are now used for sung lyrics: "*Wir fahren, fahren, fahren auf der Autobahn,*" they sing, which translates to "We drive, drive, drive on the autobahn." The phonetic commonality between the thrice-repeated "*fahren, fahren, fahren*" and "fun, fun, fun" has been picked out by many listeners, believing it to be Kraftwerk's spin on the Beach Boys' 1964 song "Fun, Fun, Fun," but that was clarified by Wolfgang Flür to only have been a coincidence: "That is wrong. But it works. Driving is fun. We had no speed limit on the autobahn, we could race through the highways, through the Alps, so yes, fahren fahren fahren, fun fun fun. But it wasn't anything to do with the Beach Boys!"[5]

It's a happy accident all the same, and feels like Kraftwerk—like so many krautrock musicians before them—were consciously creating a new German music by using American music for their own means. Whereas the original Beach Boys song helped define the California myth, Kraftwerk's "Autobahn" helped illustrate the German reality. Hütter described the song as a "sound painting," and that is exactly what it is, a marvel of little melodies and bouncing drums that paints a picture of what it feels like to drive on the autobahn, experiencing the wind, rush, and fun.[6] The song feels like the main influence on the KLF's ambient road trip album *Chill Out* many years later.

Ironically, the Beach Boys were an influence on the band, albeit in a far more oblique way. In an interview with *Rock & Folk*, Hütter made that point that "In a hundred years from now, when people want to know what California was like in the '60s, they only have to listen to a single by the Beach Boys."[7] For a more modern German equivalent, the band turned to the autobahn.

The German highway that the Kraftwerk song romanticizes was originally conceived in the 1920s, but progress was slow as construction of the first segment only began in 1929. When Hitler came to power as Chancellor of the Third Reich in 1933, he greatly increased efforts to construct the autobahn, completing 2,400 miles before further construction was halted due to the war effort in 1941. However, the construction of the autobahn created another problem, which was that only the wealthy owned vehicles to populate this massive highway. Thus, in 1934, Hitler ordered the production of an affordable vehicle by Volkswagen, whose name is a compound word literally translating to the "People's Car."

Kraftwerk's toying with symbols that could be traced back to Hitler drew some criticism, which Ralf Hütter clarified in an interview with *Media för Musiker*:

Our roots were in the culture that was stopped by Hitler; the school of Bauhaus, German Expressionism. We didn't have musical influences. One was Stockhausen, one of the pioneers of electronic music. We felt somehow that the age of composed music had passed and we strived for simpler music, something that could be played on the radio without having to be adjusted to current styles of music.[8]

After *Autobahn*, Kraftwerk shifted again on *Radio-Activity*, infusing soul into their synths and grooves into their drum programing to produce a far more melodic and song-based album and then refining that approach to create three bona fide masterpieces in 1977's *Trans-Europe Express*, 1978's *Man-Machine*, and 1981's *Computer World*. These are their best albums, but they are also not really krautrock, and would be better saved for discussion in a 33 1/3 book on synth-pop.

Released in 1977, *Trans-Europe Express* represents the symbolic death of krautrock: no longer interested in Germany, Kraftwerk was now traveling across Europe, moving off the autobahn and onto the Trans-Europe Express railway. By 1977, most of the big krautrock bands were barely holding on. Rosko Gee and Rebop Kwaku Baah had just joined Can, slowly edging out founding member Holger Czukay and marking the turning point in which the band no longer pushed the envelope. Faust, Harmonia, and Neu! were all no more. Hans-Joachim Roedelius was looking to start his own solo career, and Cluster briefly disbanded. Amon Düül II was still active, but their golden days were well behind them. Tangerine Dream was becoming an album factory, never reaching the heights of their Virgin days. If 1968 was the year that krautrock began, then 1977—exactly a decade later—can be considered its end.

13 Off the Autobahn and onto the Trans-Europe Express: Krautrock's Legacy

Krautrock's appeal was not limited to Germany, nor was it treated as a mere curiosity by music listeners outside that region. In fact, krautrock has been celebrated by artists and unrelated genres to the point that it has become well-integrated into the music bloodstream.

Krautrock has had no more devout a champion than David Bowie. In August 1975, Bowie proclaimed that "rock and roll is dead," likening it to "a toothless old woman."[1] Statements such as these were hyperbolic and meant to shock audiences, but clearly Bowie believed it: he had already left the glam rock that made him famous behind, switching to blue-eyed soul with *Young Americans*, released months before the interview, while looking for his next reinvention.

He found that reinvention in this new, electrifying music being made in Germany, and Bowie-fied the krautrock sound on *Station to Station*, regarded as a transition album between his early '70s glam rock and his artsier work in the late '70s. The ten-minute title track has the same feeling of being in transit as so many krautrock acts such as Neu! and Kraftwerk. He would go on to be one of the most vocal admirers of Neu! and La Düsseldorf.

In 1976, Bowie made confounding, cocaine-fueled comments that showed a superficial and even problematic interest in Germany, including that "Britain could benefit from a Fascist leader" and "Rock stars are fascists. Adolf Hitler was one of the first rock stars," and was even detained for possession of Nazi paraphernalia.[2] That said, the music that he soon made was anything but shallow or stupid; instead, it was deeply invested in German culture. The year 1977 saw the release of two Bowie albums, *Low* and *"Heroes,"* part of a three-album run that would be dubbed the "Berlin Trilogy," along with 1979's *Lodger*. These albums contain myriad references to Germany: "Weeping Wall" evokes the Berlin Wall, "V-2 Schneider" name-checks Kraftwerk's Florian Schneider (months after Kraftwerk themselves name-checked David Bowie and Iggy Pop on *Trans-Europe Express*), while the enduring hit "Heroes" references Neu!'s "Hero" in its title and, again, the Berlin Wall in its lyrics. But the music—fragmented, strange, and even ambient in parts—was clearly the result of a deep fascination with the groundbreaking sounds of krautrock. Bowie also wanted to collaborate with Neu! guitarist Michael Rother, which unfortunately never came to pass. Bowie also brought the Stooges' Iggy Pop with him to Germany, and a similar Germanic influence can be heard on Iggy Pop's debut solo album *The Idiot*, which Bowie helped produce. Pop would also speak very highly of Klaus Dinger's drumming on Neu!

Over ensuing years, krautrock's influence trickled down from punk rock into post-punk and eventually indie rock. The second half of *Neu! '75*, with its bracing guitar chords and unhinged vocals, would be the model for so much punk music just two years later, while Can found a fan in the most unlikely of people, the Sex Pistols' John Lydon, who considered *Tago Mago* "stunning." The Fall came after, a post-punk outlet that had a notable, inimitable style of Spartan, tribal drumming and spoken vocals from its leader Mark E. Smith, whose words themselves seemed rarely to matter. In that regard, Smith clearly took after krautrock bands where the text was less important than the texture, even before Smith spelled it out clearly when he proclaimed "I Am Damo Suzuki," referencing the Can singer. In an interview, Smith would one day name-drop Can's "Vitamin C" as one of his favorite songs, thereby inspiring Portishead's Geoff Barrow to immediately purchase the record. After recording two of the most acclaimed trip-hop albums in the 1990s, Portishead went on hiatus, and when they returned in 2008, they had left trip-hop behind, changing their sound to—you guessed it—krautrock. After Portishead, Barrow would form a more straight-up krautrock band called Beak>.

Elsewhere, Sonic Youth, under the one-time alias Ciccone Youth, name-dropped Neu! on the song "Two Cool Rock Chicks Listening to Neu," later included on the 2009 Neu! tribute album, *Brand Neu!* alongside songs by Primal Scream and LCD Soundsystem. But anyone listening to Steve Shelley's drums will recognize the influence of Neu!'s motorik drumming. Shelley's hits are charged with a similar kinetic energy, sounding at times like the New York City subway. Meanwhile, Kraftwerk's UK number one hit "The Model" was covered in the most unexpected of places, the noise rock band Big Black led by indie rock producer-engineer Steve Albini, who excavated Kraftwerk's love of melody but left the synthesizers behind.

It made sense that punk rock, indie rock, and alternative rock would be fond of krautrock: these are all genres that are characterized by the inherent practitioners' belief that what was popular and mainstream and being played on the radio was not the only music out there worth listening to. But more than that, punk, indie, and krautrock also shared a DIY attitude that you didn't need to be a professional musician or have access to a state-of-the-art recording studio to make good music. In fact, there was something liberating and authentic about being removed from the status quo.

Krautrock also proved you could be radical and still achieve at least some commercial success. Can and La Düsseldorf both had unexpected hits in their own country, for example, while others such as Kraftwerk and Faust found measurable success outside Germany. And so in addition to being name-dropped by the Fall, Can would soon find themselves being covered by Radiohead and Pavement's Stephen Malkmus, while its song names would inspire the band names of Texan indie stalwarts Spoon and Montreal space rock act Yoo Doo Right. In LCD Soundsystem's breakthrough single, "Losing My Edge," James Murphy announces that "I was there in 1968, I was there at the first Can show in Cologne," even though, born in 1970, he physically couldn't have been. But it didn't matter: the cool kids had all caught onto Can, and to be cooler, you had to be there, at least in spirit. Meanwhile, the novelty of de-emphasizing rock while still using a rock beat would be picked up by artists like Stereolab and Deerhunter, while Neu!'s bass-less setup that could still pummel had been taken to heart by garage rock revivalist bands such as the Black Keys, the White Stripes, and Yeah Yeah Yeahs.

Outside of rock, Can would be remixed by artists like Brian Eno and U.N.K.L.E. on the 1997 album *Sacrilege*, and sampled by hip-hop artists such as Kanye West and A Tribe Called Quest. Even Guru Guru found themselves sampled by Danny Brown on 2016's *Atrocity Exhibition*, as the album's opening sound, in fact. Faust would later find a kindred spirit in hip-hop noisemakers Dälek, while their infamous live performances which brought in industrial tools would be picked up by industrial acts later in Einstürzende Neubauten.

Of course, that is without mentioning the pioneering electronic music of the Berlin School musicians and Kraftwerk, who popularized the use of synthesizers and drum machines, and would have immeasurable influence on electronic acts to this day. Meanwhile, before Brian Eno named it "ambient," many krautrock musicians were making quiet, beautiful, and strange music that could be retroactively tagged as such, including Can on *Future Days*, Cluster post-Harmonia, and certain Neu! songs where the beat takes the backseat.

Whereas a genre like Britpop was hyper-national and—with rare exception—distinctly a phenomenon isolated to its native country, krautrock was transnational. Many of its practitioners like Agitation Free, Can, and Embryo were making a new musical language by assimilating sounds from across the globe. This certainly helped krautrock break through outside of Germany and subsequently influence countless global artists, scenes, and genres. To listen to krautrock decades later is to still hear the future.

10 Essential Tracks

1 Can – "Paperhouse"

2 Neu! – "Für Immer"

3 Amon Düül II – Eye-Shaking King"

4 Faust – "It's a Rainy Day, Sunshine Girl"

5 Harmonia – "Walky-Talky"

6 Cluster – "Sowiesoso"

7 Popol Vuh – "Kyrie"

8 Tangerine Dream – "Phaedra"

9 Ashra – "Sunrain"

10 Kraftwerk – "Autobahn"

Notes

Introduction

1 Steve Hanson, "Damo Suzuki," *Terrascope*, 2002.

2 Jason Gross, "John Weinzierl Interview," *Perfect Sound Forever*, August 2008.

3 Frank Gingeleit, "The Drumming Man: An Interview with Mani Neumeier of Guru Guru," *Aural Innovations*, April 2002.

4 David Stubbs, *Future Days: Krautrock and the Building of Modern Germany* (London: Faber & Faber, 2014).

5 Jan Reetze, *Times & Sounds: Germany's Journey from Jazz and Pop to Krautrock and Beyond* (Bremen: Halvmall, 2020).

6 Douglas Botting, *In the Ruins of the Reich* (London: Methuen, 2012).

7 Gregory Gethard, "The German Economic Miracle," Investopedia, June 29, 2021.

8 Gethard, "German Economic Miracle."

9 Christian Monson, "The Myth That the Marshall Plan Rebuilt Germany's Economy after WWII," *Fee*, March 19, 2022.

10 Harald Jahner, *Aftermath: Life in the Fallout of the Third Reich* (London: WH Allen, 2022).

11 Monson, "Myth That the Marshall Plan."

12 Jahner, *Aftermath*.

13 Dwight D. Eisenhower, "Eisenhower's Orders on Germany," *Current History* 7, no. 3 (1944): 412–15.

14 Manfred Knapp, Wolfgang F. Stolper, and Michael Hudson, "Reconstruction and West-Integration: The Impact of the Marshall Plan on Germany," *Zeitschrift Für Die Gesamte Staatswissenschaft / Journal of Institutional and Theoretical Economics* 137, no. 3 (1981): 415–33.

15 Gross, "John Weinzierl Interview."

16 Tim Barr, *Kraftwerk: From Düsseldorf to the Future (with Love)* (London: Ebury Digital, 2013).

17 Eothen Alapatt, "Cluster," *Red Bull Music Academy*, 2010.

18 Chris May, "Tangerine Dream's Peter Baumann on Synth Improvisation and Studio Wizardry," *The Vinyl Factory*, July 8, 2019.

19 Reetze, *Times & Sounds*.

1 Future Days: CAN

1 Damon Krukowski, "Ptolemaic," *Terrascope*, 1998.

2 Rob Young and Irmin Schmidt, *All Gates Open: The Story of Can* (London: Faber & Faber, 2018), p. 43.

3 Young and Schmidt, *All Gates Open*.

4 A. Warner, *Can's Tago Mago* (New York: Bloomsbury Academic, 2015).

5 David Stubbs, "Can's Jaki Liebezeit: The Man Who Marched to the Beat of His Own Drum," *The Guardian*, January 23, 2017.

6 Ben Graham, "Still Growing: Hans-Joachim Irmler and Jaki Liebezeit Interviewed," *The Quietus*, July 2, 2015.

7 Stubbs, *Future Days*.

8 Young and Schmidt, *All Gates Open*.

9 Young and Schmidt, *All Gates Open*.

10 Rob Hughes, "The Prog Interview: Can's Damo Suzuki," November 3, 2016.

11 Hughes, "Prog Interview."

12 Simon Reynolds, "Pavement Interview," *Melody Maker*, 1992.

13 Hanson, "Damo Suzuki."

14 Young and Schmidt, *All Gates Open*.

15 Holger Czukay, "Holger Czukay—Movies." *Discogs*, n.d.

2 The German Beatles: Faust

1 John Doran, "Faust and Last and Always: Germany's Most Radical Rock Group Talk," *The Quietus*, June 16, 2010.

2 Alexis Petridis, "Krautrock Legends Faust: 'We Were Naked and Stoned a Lot—and We Ate Dog Food,'" *The Guardian*, October 18, 2021.

3 Klemen Breznikar, "Faust | Interview | Jean-Hervé Peron | 'One of the Famous Unknowns,'" *It's Psychedelic Baby! Magazine*, May 8, 2011.

4 Petridis, "Krautrock Legends Faust."

5 Doran, "Faust and Last and Always."

6 Petridis, "Krautrock Legends Faust."

7   Breznikar, "Faust | Interview | Jean-Hervé Peron |."

8   Jean-Hervé Péron, "Arnulf Meifert," *Faust Pages*, December 2004.

9   Breznikar, "Faust | Interview | Jean-Hervé Peron |."

10 Melody Maker, "Deleted: LP That Was TOO Popular," *Faust Pages*, 1972.

11 Breznikar, "Faust | Interview | Jean-Hervé Peron |."

12 Albert Freeman, "Drone and Dusted: Tony Conrad Interviewed," *The Quietus*, April 9, 2016.

13 Freeman, "Drone and Dusted."

14 Freeman, "Drone and Dusted."

15 Breznikar, "Faust | Interview | Jean-Hervé Peron |."

16 Stubbs, *Future Days*.

17 Breznikar, "Faust | Interview | Jean-Hervé Peron |."

18 *Frequency*, "INTERVIEW: Jim O'Rourke," *Frequency #1*, 1996.

19 Dominique Leone, "Derbe Respect, Alder," *Pitchfork*, May 10, 2004.

3 Out of the City and into the Forst: Cluster and Harmonia

1   David Stubbs, "'Free Playing, Free Life': The Zodiak Free Arts Lab and the Rise of the German Avant-Garde," *Red Bull Music Academy*, September 5, 2018.

2   Klemen Breznikar, "Hans-Joachim Roedelius Interview about Kluster and Beyond," *It's Psychedelic Baby! Magazine*, December 10, 2011.

3   Stubbs, "Free Playing, Free Life."

4   Stubbs, "Free Playing, Free Life."

5   Alapatt, "Cluster."

6   Alapatt, "Cluster."

7   David Stubbs, "A Raging Peace: The Strange World of …
    Hans-Joachim Roedelius," *The Quietus*, October 9, 2018.

8   Rob Young, "Dieter Moebius (1944–2015)," *Artforum*,
    December 28, 2015.

9   Stubbs, *Future Days*.

10 Geeta Dayal, "Harmonia," *Harmonia*, n.d.; and Stubbs, *Future
    Days*.

11 Stubbs, *Future Days*.

12 Matt Beck, "Brian Eno and Discreet Music," *The Curator*,
    February 27, 2009.

4 Marmalade Skies: Tangerine Dream

1   Don Snowdon, "Robert Moog: 'I Wouldn't Call This Music'—A
    Classic Interview to Mark a Google Doodle," *The Guardian*,
    May 23, 2012.

2   Janey Roberts, "Why Queen Should Not Have Printed 'No
    Synthesizers' on Liner Notes," *Classic Rock History*, n.d.

3   Ben Hewitt, "Our Band's Not Electric: Edgar Froese from
    Tangerine Dream Interviewed," *The Quietus*, March 12, 2010.

4   Ulrich Adelt, *Krautrock: German Music in the Seventies* (Ann
     Arbor, MI: University of Michigan Press, 2016); and Deutsches
     Museum, "Tangerine Dream: The Power of Cosmic Sounds,"
     Google Arts & Culture, n.d.

5   Hewitt, "Our Band's Not Electric."

6   *The Quietus*, "Play as If Your Life Depends on It: Tangerine
     Dream In 1970," *The Quietus*, May 11, 2008.

7   Deutsches Museum, "Tangerine Dream."

8   Reetze, *Times & Sounds*.

9   May, "Tangerine Dream's Peter Baumann."

10   John Clarkson, "Thorsten Quaeschning—Interview,"
     Pennyblackmusic, June 29, 2018.

5 The Ancient Heavenly Connection: Ash Ra Tempel

1   Robert Barry, "'Everything Was in the Moment': An Interview
     with Manuel Göttsching," *The Quietus*, March 7, 2017.

2   Archie Patterson, "Ash Ra Tempel: An Interview with Manuel
     Göttsching," *Eurock*, n.d.

3   Kosmische Musik Group, "An Interview with Manuel
     Göttsching (2002)," Ashra, 2002.

4   Tristan Gatward, "The Story of E2–E4—Manuel
     Göttsching's Accidental Masterpiece," *Loud and Quiet*,
     June 6, 2019.

6 Haunted Island: Agitation Free

1   Marshall Gu, "An Interview with Lutz Graf-Ulbrich," September 18, 2022.

2   Gu, "Interview with Lutz Graf-Ulbrich."

3   Klemen Breznikar, "Agitation Free Interview with Lutz Graf-Ulbrich," *It's Psychedelic Baby! Magazine*, December 19, 2018.

4   Michael Freerix, "Music Was Our Adventure," *Perfect Sound Forever*, October 2007.

5   Gu, "Interview with Lutz Graf-Ulbrich."

6   Gu, "Interview with Lutz Graf-Ulbrich."

7   Breznikar, "Agitation Free Interview with Lutz Graf-Ulbrich."

8   Gu, "Interview with Lutz Graf-Ulbrich."

9   Gu, "Interview with Lutz Graf-Ulbrich."

10 Gu, "Interview with Lutz Graf-Ulbrich."

11 Gu, "Interview with Lutz Graf-Ulbrich."

7 Electric Junk: Guru Guru

1   Klemen Breznikar, "Guru Guru Interview with Mani Neumeier," *It's Psychedelic Baby! Magazine*, January 28, 2019.

2   Marshall Gu, "An Interview with Ax Genrich," October 2022.

3   John O'Regan, "Guru Guru," *Terrascope*, August 1995.

4   Breznikar, "Guru Guru Interview."

5   Klemen Breznikar, "Gila," *It's Psychedelic Baby! Magazine*, April 19, 2020.

8 Universal Believer: Popol Vuh

1   Archie Patterson, "Florian Fricke Interview," *Eurock*, n.d.

2   Patterson, "Florian Fricke Interview."

3   Reetze, *Times & Sounds*.

4   Werner Herzog and Paul Cronin, *Herzog on Herzog* (London: Faber & Faber, 2007).

5   Paul Cronin, *Werner Herzog—A Guide for the Perplexed: Conversations with Paul Cronin* (London: Faber & Faber, 2014).

6   Patterson, "Florian Fricke Interview."

7   Patterson, "Florian Fricke Interview."

8   Jason Gross, "Popol Vuh Interview," *Perfect Sound Forever*, August 2013.

9 Made in Germany: Amon Düül II

1   Will Hodgkinson, "Even Hippies Need a Toilet Door," *The Guardian*, November 16, 2007.

2   Gross, "John Weinzierl Interview."

3   Gross, "John Weinzierl Interview."

4   Reetze, *Times & Sounds*.

5   Adelt, *Krautrock*.

6   Gross, "John Weinzierl Interview."

7   As quoted in Reetze, *Times & Sounds*.

8   Gross, "John Weinzierl Interview."

9 Gross, "John Weinzierl Interview."

10 Reetze, *Times & Sounds*.

11 Andy Whittaker, "Amon Düül II—Yeti Talks to Yogi," *Delerium's Psychedelic Web*, 1997.

12 Whittaker, "Amon Düül II."

13 Gross, "John Weinzierl Interview."

14 Reetze, *Times & Sounds*.

15 Edwin Pouncy, "Amon Düül II: Communing with Chaos," *The Wire 144*, February 1996.

10 World Fusion: Embryo

1 Klemen Breznikar, "Embryo Interview with Christian Burchard," *It's Psychedelic Baby Magazine*, December 12, 2011.

2 Breznikar, "Embryo Interview."

3 Breznikar, "Embryo Interview."

4 Breznikar, "Embryo Interview."

5 Klemen Breznikar, "Roman Bunka Interview," *It's Psychedelic Baby Magazine*, May 8, 2019.

6 Abdul Malek, "Embryo 'We Keep On,'" *Rising Storm* [Review], 1973.

7 Marshall Gu, "An Interview with Marja Burchard," September 26, 2022.

8 *Bandcamp*, "Auf Auf," *Bandcamp*, n.d.

9 Gu, "Interview with Marja Burchard."

10 Gu, "Interview with Marja Burchard."

11 Gu, "Interview with Marja Burchard."

11 A Beat That Lasts Für Immer: NEU!

1 Biba Kopf, "Unedited Klaus Dinger," *The Wire*, March 2020.

2 Adelt, *Krautrock*.

3 Jason Gross, "Michael Rother Interview," *Perfect Sound Forever*, March 1998.

4 David Stubbs, "Klaus Dinger and Me: Miki Yui of Japandorf Interviewed," *The Quietus*, April 5, 2013.

5 Kopf, "Unedited Klaus Dinger."

6 Kopf, "Unedited Klaus Dinger."

7 Gross, "Michael Rother Interview."

8 Biba Kopf, "Michael Rother Interview Transcript," *The Wire*, 2001.

9 Gross, "Michael Rother Interview."

10 Gross, "Michael Rother Interview."

11 Kopf, "Michael Rother Interview."

12 Kopf, "Michael Rother Interview."

13 Kopf, "Michael Rother Interview."

14 Kopf, "Unedited Klaus Dinger."

15 Kopf, "Michael Rother Interview."

16 Stubbs, "Klaus Dinger and Me."

17 Pierre Perrone, "Klaus Dinger: Pioneer of the 'Motorik' Beat," *Independent*, April 10, 2008.

12 We Are the Robots: Kraftwerk

1   Frank Doris, "The Incalculable Influence of Kraftwerk," *Copper*, March 22, 2022; and Visit Düsseldorf, "The Legend of Kraftwerk," Google Arts & Culture, n.d.

2   As quoted in M. Schiller, *Soundtracking Germany Popular Music and National Identity* (Lanham, MD: Rowman and Littlefield International, 2020).

3   Markus Weisbeck, "The Model," *Frieze*, August 21, 2015.

4   Stubbs, *Future Days*.

5   Dave Thompson, "Autobahn," AllMusic, n.d.

6   Tim Jonze, "Kraftwerk's Ralf Hütter: 'Music Is about Intensity . . . the Rest Is Just Noise,'" *The Guardian*, 2017.

7   John Doran, "From Neu! To Kraftwerk: Football, Motorik, and the Pulse of Modernity," *The Quietus*, May 6, 2020.

8   Barr, *Kraftwerk*.

13 Off the Autobahn and onto the Trans-Europe Express: Krautrock's Legacy

1   Anthony O'Grady, "Classic David Bowie Interview: Adolf Hitler and the Need for a New Right," *The Quietus*, January 25, 2010.

2   Paul Sorene, "That David Bowie 'Nazi Salute' and Eric Clapton's 'Wogs' Created Rock against Racism," *Flashback*, 2014.